# FINISHING WELL

## In life and ministry

### God's Protection From Burnout

# BILL MILLS & CRAIG PARRO

Leadership Resources International

Palos Heights • Illinois

Fourth Printing: February 2003

THIS MINISTRY IS DEDICATED TO:

The Glory of God
The Honor of His Word
The Building Up of the Body of Christ

*We proclaim him, admonishing and teaching everyone with all wisdom, so that we may present everyone perfect in Christ. To this end I labor, struggling with all his energy, which so powerfully works in me.*

*Colossians 1:28,29*

# Table of Contents

**Section 3—The Pathway to Life:**
            **Experiencing God's Keeping Grace**

# Foreword *by*
# **Dr. Ron Cline**

*President, HCJB World Radio*

I first met Bill Mills in the late 1970's when he came to the English Fellowship Church in Quito, Ecuador, South America to hold a week long conference. It was the first conference I had tried after becoming the pastor and I was concerned that he would be teaching some pretty high-powered people, some of them long-time mission - aries, others from the Embassy community and still others from the business world. The bond that tied us together was worshiping in the English language. The spectrum of biblical knowledge was very broad, from no previous church attendance to Bible trained missionaries.

I will never forget the impact this man's presentations made on me. There were no, "I think..." or "It seems to me..."—only "Look with me and see what the Bible says...". Night after night, point after point, no flash, no show, just rock-bottom truth. It affected my personal ministry and it affected the lives of the people there.

I met Craig shortly after he joined Bill's ministry and together they built Leadership Resources. I was taken immediately by his commitment to help others and his desire to cooperate.

Since that time, Bill, Craig and our people have been able to partner in several areas of the world through their ministry of Leadership Resources. It is basically that...to equip local pastors and church workers, many with no formal training, with Bibles and books, with study skills and preaching skills to build Christ's Church throughout Latin America and beyond.

What a thrill to be able to hand off to them a vision I had and watch them build it to a wonderful ministry world wide. Their vision and reputation for giving, asking nothing in return, have brought invitations to do the same ministry around the world.

Only Eternity will know the impact these men have had on the Church of the world.

Now they have co-authored a book, this one with a two part title. The first part says, "Finishing well in life and ministry...". I cannot think of one person in ministry who should not have this as a priority. Our prayers during these days of temptation and failure should be, "Lord, help me finish well!" That has to include our lives, our families and our ministries.

Some years ago I wrote out a prayer that has been put to music, "I want to be faithful, I want to be true. I want to be faithful, your will to do. And with my life, Lord, I want to serve you. I want to be faithful, I want to be new!"

Bottom line, "Lord, let me finish well."

The second part of the title is, "God's protection from burnout". Burnout is not new. This book will illustrate how it touched Elijah, Moses, Peter, David...so many of our biblical heros. It touches us. What Bill and Craig have done is help us to learn from Scripture, from the real life situations that these men of the faith experienced, and apply them to our lives. There are principles here that will save your ministries, your marriages, maybe your lives.

This is a must read for anyone in ministry. Read and reread this book. Give it to your pastor, to your staff, use it in your families.

I am proud to say that I know these men and to tell you that they practice what they preach.

May God bless us all as we strive to finish well.

Dr. Ron Cline
June 1998

*Therefore, since through God's mercy we have this ministry, we do not lose heart.*

*2 Corinthians 4:1*

# Introduction

Pastors, church leaders and missionaries are facing great battles in the ministry during these days, and many are losing heart. The attacks are both from within and without. We know all too well our own weaknesses and inconsistencies. No one has to tell us that we are not sufficient for the great work set before us. Lest we forget, Satan is quick to remind us of our inadequacies as he tears away at our hearts.

The external pressures are just as great. The culture in which we live undermines our labors and delights when one of us stum - bles. Our own people confront us with a host of expectations which are far more than we can deliver. With salary levels that are often marginal at best, simply providing adequately for our families becomes yet another battlefront. Of course, our families face their own struggles and pain, looking to us for understanding, affirma - tion and answers.

Ministry is proving to be considerably more expensive than originally thought. It is exacting a terrible price. It is costing us our lives. Many of God's choicest servants are burning out and giving up in the process.

In *Pastors at Risk*, H.B. London and Neil B. Wiseman quote from a 1991 survey of pastors conducted by the Fuller Institute for Church Growth. They list these striking statistics as risk factors for pastors:

- 90% of pastors work more than 46 hours a week
- 80% believed that pastoral ministry affected their families nega - tively
- 33% said that being in ministry was an outright hazard to their family
- 75% reported a significant stress-related crisis at least once in their ministry
- 50% felt unable to meet the needs of the job
- 90% felt they were inadequately trained to cope with ministry demands
- 70% say they have a lower self-esteem now than when they started out
- 40% reported a serious conflict with a parishioner at least once a month
- 37% confessed having been involved in inappropriate sexual behavior with someone in the church
- 70% do not have someone they consider a close friend

*1991 Survey of Pastors*[1]
*Fuller Institute of Church Growth*

---

1  H.B. London, Jr. & Neil B. Wiseman, *Pastors at Risk*, Victor Books, /S.P. Publications, Inc., U.S.A., 1993, p. 22.

## THE KEY TO THE BATTLE

We as church leaders battle a host of enemies. How are we to survive this onslaught, let alone flourish in the ministry? Fortunately, the Scriptures give us great hope! The answers are rooted in God Himself and in our experience of His sustaining presence. We will discover in *Battling Burnout in the Ministry* that the key to life and ministry is found in our view of God, our view of ourselves and in our view of ministry. This book will present a greater vision of God in His glory and sovereignty. We will be reminded that all of our fullness and sufficiency is in Christ. We will discover that effective, enduring ministry is grounded in that which God is doing, those eternal works which He is fulfilling, in part, through us. We will see that our personal identity, our adequacy, flows out of our "in Christ" experience.

The premise of this book is that the terrible disease of *burnout* is not primarily the result of our unfortunate circumstances. It is not a function of our lack of resources or planning, nor the result of our own failings and weaknesses. *Burnout* is largely a spiritual problem rooted in our theology, for the battles rage primarily in our hearts and minds. By theology, we are referring to more than our creedal orthodoxy. It is our practical theology in daily living which reveals what we *really* believe.

In his very challenging book *God in the Wasteland* , David Wells talks of the "weightlessness of God."

> *It is one of the defining marks of Our Time that God is now weightless. I do not mean by this that he is ethereal but rather that he has become unimportant. He rests upon the world so inconsequentially as not to be noticeable. He has lost his saliency for human life. Those who assure the pollsters of their belief in God's existence may nonetheless consider him less interesting than television, his com - mands less authoritative than their appetites for affluence*

*and influence, his judgment no more awe-inspiring than the evening news, and his truth less compelling than the advertisers' sweet fog of flattery and lies. That is weight - lessness.*[2]

We can readily affirm that this is taking place in our society. But the view of a "weightless God" has also deeply affected us in the ministry. We so desire to be relevant and to meet the needs of our culture. But in the process, even among the clergy, our view of God has been lessened, so that we now worship what Wells calls a "diminished God."

A diminished God will not be able to keep the hearts of those whom He has called to serve Him. It is our prayer that as we seek an exalted God, lifted high in His sovereignty, His holiness, His glory, power and grace, that we might be transformed in His presence and our hearts sustained in Him.

This book is about theology and about what we think and believe, but it is not intended to operate on merely a theological or intellectual level. If it does so, then we have failed as authors. The material we are presenting is devotional in style. Laced throughout are the applicable truths which can bring us very practical help along the way. However, the strong encouragement that we desire to bring is God Himself. We are convinced that all of our lives and ministries flow out of the way in which we see God. As our vision of God becomes greater, our hearts will become freer and our ministries will grow fuller. We will be continually coming back to God, seeking Him for His eternal resources, which alone can sustain us from day to day.

---

2 David F. Wells, *God in the Wasteland - The Reality of Truth in a World of Fading Dreams*, Wm. B. Eerdmans Publishing Co., Grand Rapids, MI, 1994, p. 88.

## BURNOUT IS INEVITABLE, UNLESS...

H.B. London and Neil B. Wiseman, in their excellent book *Your Pastor Is an Endangered Species* , say, "Burnout is increasing among pastors these days. It is caused by too much stress carried for too long without relief."[3] We are defining "*burnout* in the ministry" as the point at which a pastor, church leader or mission - ary gives up, unable or unwilling to continue in the ministry. Of course, each of us in the ministry experiences periods during which we are tired, frustrated and even depressed. Thoughts of leaving the ministry come to us all. However, by God's grace we are able to endure these "short term" burnout experiences. *Burnout,* as we are studying it here, is losing heart so completely that we cannot continue. The truth is, too many of us are very close to that point.

We began this project realizing that *burnout* in the ministry is a terrible problem today. We knew that many of our brothers and sisters struggle with *burnout* and that some would fall. Although we wanted to bring some help from the Scriptures to encourage their hearts, the more we studied God's Word and talked with pastors, missionaries and denominational leaders, the more we realized how wrong we were. Not only is *burnout* a widespread problem today, in fact, *burnout* is inevitable! In addition to our own weaknesses, we face pressures, demands and expectations, as well as battles with Satan; as a result, every one of us will burn out unless God is there, present with us in the ministry.

*Therefore, since through God's mercy we have this ministry, we do not lose heart. (2 Corinthians 4:1)*

---

3 H.B. London, Jr. & Neil B. Wiseman, *Your Pastor Is an Endangered Species*, Victor Books/S.P. Publications, Inc., U.S.A., 1996, p. 63.

The glory of His presence becomes all of our hope. God is the source of our lives, our call, and our ministries. We are not here because of our skills, our eloquence, our brilliance, or our poten - tial, but because of God's mercy. Only His mercies, which are new every morning, can sustain us in the ministry. May our Father encourage your heart as you meditate with us on these Scriptures. We trust that this book will be part of His mercies toward you. May God become your keeper, His glory your only goal, and His joy your strength.

Bill Mills
Craig Parro
January 1997

# SECTION 1

# The Glory of His Presence: Ministering out of the Overflow

*You have made known to me the path of life; you will fill me with joy in your presence, with eternal pleasures at your right hand.*

*Psalms 16:11*

*The LORD said, "Go out and stand on the mountain in the presence of the LORD, for the LORD is about to pass by." Then a great and powerful wind tore the mountains apart and shattered the rocks before the LORD, but the LORD was not in the wind. After the wind there was an earthquake, but the LORD was not in the earthquake.*

*1 Kings 19:11*

# 1

## Elijah:
## When We Are Alone,
## God Comes to Us

Among all of the prophets God has called to stand before Him and His people, Elijah was the most powerful. We see in him great strength of character, boldness in the face of political opposition, courage before great enemies, and a depth of faith that inspires us. Yet when James wants to encourage our hearts in prayer and stimulate our faith, he tells us Elijah was "just like us."

> *Elijah was a man just like us. He prayed earnestly that it would not rain, and it did not rain on the land for three and a half years. Again he prayed, and the heavens gave rain, and the earth produced its crops. (James 5:17,18)*

Elijah, too, was made out of dust. He had a nature just like ours. When he prayed, his prayers were powerful before the Lord. When we are clothed in the righteousness of Jesus Christ, God's Son, and walk openly before the Lord and before one another, we also stand before the God of heaven with that same great power because of His grace.

Elijah was the most powerful prophet who ever lived, and yet he was just like you and me. To protect us from burning out in the ministry, we learn from him that the practical necessities of rest, diet and shelter are critical if we are to be sustained; that "alone-ness" in the work can be devastating; and that God provides co–workers to help us and encourage our hearts. Most of all, we learn that unless God comes to us in the midst of our work, our battles and our vulnerabilities, surrounding us with His presence, we will not make it.

## HIDE YOURSELF, ELIJAH

In the book of 1 Kings, we see one of the most incredible scenes in all of Scripture as Elijah, filled with the power of God, confronted King Ahab, Queen Jezebel, 450 priests of Baal and 400 prophets of Asherah. Ahab, the wicked king of Israel, and his family followed the Baals, and the 400 prophets of Asherah ate at Jezebel's table. Jezebel, daughter of the king of Sidon, led Ahab's heart further from the Lord by encouraging him to build a temple and set up an altar for Baal in Samaria. God's anger at Ahab was great.

> *Ahab also made an Asherah pole and did more to provoke the LORD, the God of Israel, to anger than did all the kings of Israel before him. (1 Kings 16:33)*

Because of Ahab's apparent limitless capacity for depravity and the way he was leading God's people astray, God pronounced a harsh judgment upon both the king and the land through His prophet Elijah.

*Now Elijah the Tishbite, from Tishbe in Gilead, said to Ahab, "As the LORD, the God of Israel, lives, whom I serve, there will be neither dew nor rain in the next few years except at my word." (1 Kings 17:1)*

God knew the anger that would fill Ahab's heart at the word of the prophet, so he told Elijah to hide himself. God would provide for him and care for his needs.

*So he did what the LORD had told him. He went to the Kerith Ravine, east of the Jordan, and stayed there. The ravens brought him bread and meat in the morning and bread and meat in the evening, and he drank from the brook. (1 Kings 17:5,6)*

God's judgment on Ahab and the nation of Israel was severe; the famine was devastating to Ahab's kingdom, but God personally cared for Elijah. He not only fed him by means of the ravens, but when the brook dried up, the Lord provided for him through a widow.

*Some time later the brook dried up because there had been no rain in the land. Then the word of the LORD came to him: "Go at once to Zarephath of Sidon and stay there. I have commanded a widow in that place to supply you with food." (1 Kings 17:7-9)*

Not only did our Father use the widow to provide food for Elijah, He used Elijah to provide for her. By God's miraculous power her flour and oil did not run out until the years of famine were over. When her son died, God again used Elijah to raise him to life.

## SHOW YOURSELF, ELIJAH

In the third year of the famine, God told Elijah to present himself before Ahab. God had led him to hide in the ravine at Kerith for over two years, but now was the time to show himself before the wicked king of Israel. Elijah was God's servant, ministering on His timetable. There was a time to hide in God and His provisions, and there was a time to stand before His people and the enemies of Israel.

So it is with you and me. God has a sovereign timetable for our lives and our ministries. Just as there are times when we are to hide ourselves in God and His provisions for us, times to be strengthened in Him and to know of His gracious care for us, there are also times to stand in His power before our people and before the enemies of His kingdom. However, just as with Elijah, we must know that we cannot stand until we have first hidden ourselves in God. It is in those times of intimacy with God through fellowship with Him in His Word and through prayer that we are strengthened for the daily battles we face.

This was Elijah's time to stand before Ahab and announce that God would send rain on the land. Surely this act of obedience before the Lord took great courage on Elijah's part, as Jezebel was killing the Lord's prophets and Ahab had abandoned the Lord. When Elijah presented himself before Ahab, the king made this incredible statement:

> *When he saw Elijah, he said to him, "Is that you, you troubler of Israel?" (1 Kings 18:17)*

It is a long-standing tradition for politicians to blame the problems they have caused on someone else! The famine in Israel was the result of Ahab's depravity before the Lord, but he "blamed the messenger" for his nation's troubles rather than taking respon - sibility for his own sins. Elijah confronted Ahab with his stubborn and rebellious heart.

> *"I have not made trouble for Israel," Elijah replied. "But you and your father's family have. You have abandoned the Lord's com- mands and have followed the Baals." (1 Kings 18:18)*

24

## ELIJAH CONFRONTS HUNDREDS OF FALSE PROPHETS

Elijah challenged Ahab to assemble the 450 prophets of Baal and the 400 prophets of Asherah on Mt. Carmel for a confrontation between the forces of darkness and the powers of light. Elijah's motivation was clear. He wanted God's chosen people to either commit to the God who had called and delivered them, or to the Baals who had captured their hearts.

> *Elijah went before the people and said, "How long will you waver between two opinions? If the LORD is God, follow him; but if Baal is God, follow him." But the people said nothing. (1 Kings 18:21)*

Elijah was strong and confrontive before Israel, but as the Scriptures continue, we see the seeds of his vulnerability to *burn-out*. He had a view of himself that was not based in reality. He had assumed a responsibility before God and His people that was out of proportion to God's call. Elijah felt that he was the only one left in all of Israel to defend God's name.

> *Then Elijah said to them, "I am the only one of the Lord's prophets left, but Baal has four hundred and fifty prophets."*
> *(1 Kings 18:22)*

We can vividly picture the familiar scene that follows. Elijah had the Israelites prepare two bulls for sacrifice. They would choose one and place it on the altar without lighting the wood on fire. The prophets of Baal would call upon their god; Elijah would call upon his God; the God who answered by fire would be recognized as the one true God.

Elijah allowed the priests of Baal to seek their god first, and they danced, shouted and cried to him from morning until noon. Midday passed, and when the time for the evening sacrifice came, their god had not yet answered with fire. The priests of Baal even slashed themselves with swords, but they were unable to awaken their god. Elijah began to taunt them.

> *At noon Elijah began to taunt them. "Shout louder!" he said. "Surely he is a god! Perhaps he is deep in thought, or busy, or traveling. Maybe he is sleeping and must be awakened."*
> *(1 Kings 18:27)*

Then the prophet of God called the people to repair the altar of the Lord, and Elijah took twelve stones representing the twelve tribes of Israel and built an altar in God's Name. He arranged the wood, cut the bull in pieces, and placed it on the altar; he soaked the entire sacrifice again and again with water and called upon the Name of the Lord. God answered with fire! The people of God were transformed as God displayed His great power and the reality of His life in the face of the empty and impotent gods they had served.

> *When all the people saw this, they fell prostrate and cried, "The LORD—he is God! The LORD—he is God!" (1 Kings 18:39)*

Elijah then commanded the people to seize the prophets of Baal and slaughter them. The children of Israel were obedient and destroyed those who had drawn their hearts away from the one true God. In His mercy, God then provided the desperately needed rain.

## ELIJAH RUNS FROM ONE WOMAN

When Ahab told Jezebel what Elijah had done, she was livid! She set her heart on destroying the prophet. After the incredibly pow - erful confrontation with the priests of Baal and the powers of darkness, what could one woman do to Elijah? Surely he would stand in God's strength in her presence as well. However, he ran for his life! He came to Beersheba, left his servant there, went a day's journey into the desert, sat under a broom tree and pleaded with God to take his life. From the incredible "high" of the battle on Mt. Carmel, Elijah sank into a depression that left him suicidal. Elijah was burned out; the great prophet had lost heart.

> *Elijah was afraid and ran for his life. When he came to Beersheba in Judah, he left his servant there, while he himself went a day's journey into the desert. He came to a broom tree, sat down under it and prayed that he might die. "I have had enough, LORD," he said. "Take my life; I am no better than my ancestors." Then he lay down under the tree and fell asleep. All at once an angel touched him and said, "Get up and eat." (1 Kings 19:3-5)*

God did not abandon His prophet but sent an angel to provide for him. The angel touched him, and God met Elijah at his point of immediate need.

> *He looked around, and there by his head was a cake of bread baked over hot coals, and a jar of water. He ate and drank and then lay down again. (1 Kings 19:6)*

After a time of rest, the angel of the Lord touched Elijah again. What persistent care, what relentless ministry God provided for His hurting prophet! Elijah was wounded by the effects of fear and by his own thoughts. He was interpreting his circumstances in the extreme and was unable to see God's presence. Because God knew that what Elijah was facing was beyond his own strength, He provided the resources needed for the long journey ahead.

> *The angel of the LORD came back a second time and touched him and said, "Get up and eat, for the journey is too much for you." So he got up and ate and drank. Strengthened by that food, he traveled forty days and forty nights until he reached Horeb, the mountain of God. (1 Kings 19:7,8)*

When Elijah reached Horeb, he went into a cave and slept again. How many of us who have struggled with *burnout* can identify with what we see in God's prophet? Although the exhaustion of battle and the desire to sleep consumed Elijah, God did an amazing thing.

He confronted Elijah with the hard questions of his actions and circumstances.

> *There he went into a cave and spent the night. And the word of the LORD came to him: "What are you doing here, Elijah?"*
> *(1 Kings 19:9)*

A major aspect of the battle with *burnout* is our inability to face the realities of our situation and the choices which have brought us to this place. I know a man whose ministry is dying, and in the midst of it, he too is dying. Each time I talk with him, he speaks of the lack of vision on his board and how his people do not respond. However, I see that he is unwilling to face his own weaknesses or to listen to his leaders. God graciously but strongly confronted Elijah with where he was and why he was there.

We, too, are often unwilling to ask the hard questions in life and ministry. The gracious work of God's Spirit speaks through the Scriptures, our marriage partners, and our leaders and brings us to face the realities of who we are, where we are, and why we are where we are. We need our Father to come to us, especially when we are hiding as Elijah was, and get "in our face" and ask, "What are you doing here? What are you about? What are your purposes? Why are you at this place? How did you get here?" The way in which we respond to God and His messengers at this point will greatly determine the scope and fruitfulness of our future ministry. Will we turn to face God and His probing, loving ministry of restoration, or will we retreat further into ourselves and the cave in which we are seeking shelter?

Elijah was unable to deal honestly with His Father's probing questions. He again retreated inwardly and was overwhelmed, even immobilized, by his false perceptions of himself and the need for him alone to protect God's reputation.

*He replied, "I have been very zealous for the LORD God Almighty. The Israelites have rejected your covenant, broken down your altars, and put your prophets to death with the sword. I am the only one left, and now they are trying to kill me too."*
*(1 Kings 19:10)*

## THE "PROPHET'S SYNDROME"

Elijah had become so consumed with the battle and so over-whelmed with his responsibility to vindicate God's great name and call His people back to Him that he had completely lost perspective. He needed God to remind him that He Himself was the keeper of His people and the protector of His own reputation. Later, God did reveal to Elijah that he was not alone, but that He had kept for Himself seven thousand who had not bowed their knees to Baal.

*"Yet I reserve seven thousand in Israel—all whose knees have not bowed down to Baal and all whose mouths have not kissed him." (1 Kings 19:18)*

The "prophet's syndrome" that we see revealed in Elijah is an attitude to which we are all vulnerable. We may feel alone in the battle with the forces of opposition surrounding us. Perhaps we, too, see ourselves out of proportion in God's purposes. We may see ourselves beyond the reality of God's call and the place God has given us in ministry. We alone are the ones who will raise the standard of righteousness or lead the march for truth or stand in the face of the enemy. In truth, God has not only raised up, but will keep, all those He desires to use in the building of His kingdom.

To deal with our vulnerability to the same "prophet's syndrome" with which Elijah struggled, we first need to see God as sovereign over His purposes and fully capable of fulfilling His will. We, too, need to have a view of ourselves that is not out of proportion in ministry. It is not up to us alone to protect God's reputation and to vindicate His Name. We also must be honest about our need for co-workers, for brothers and sisters to lean on in the ministry. A wise pastor will allow himself to be known by several of his elders or leaders and will be open with them about his weakness and his need for their support. He will function in a team ministry rather than serving as a "lone ranger," and he will train them to serve in this way. This not only strengthens the ministry with a multiplicity of gifts, but it also offers great protection for his own heart.

God provided a co-worker in the ministry for Elijah. His gift of Elisha was a support, an encouragement, a friend, and one who would share the burden of responsibility for God's people. If we are serving in a multi-staff mission or church, our brothers and sisters with whom we serve are gifts from the Lord's heart to us as well as those whom we are serving. If you are not in a multi-staff environment, I would encourage you to pray that God will provide a like-minded partner in the work, a friend with whom you can pray and share your burdens and your dreams. Ask God to give you someone, in addition to your marriage partner, who can walk alongside you, to whom you can be accountable, who can lift up your heart in the difficult days and share your joys when God provides great victories.

Sometimes pastors will seek a fellow pastor in the community as a brother with whom he can share his burdens, someone with whom he can pray and open his heart vulnerably. This can be a valuable ministry. Although fellowship, teaching times or conferences can also be great sources of encouragement, this can also be a "make believe" solution to a deeper problem. It may be that a pastor's views of himself and his ministry are out of proportion and that he sees himself above his elders and deacons. If he is truly on another level spiritually and authoritatively, then the leaders of his church will not be able to identify with him or minister to his heart. However, if he is a team member and sees his leaders as spiritual, mature men, then he will seek an associate pastor or a board member to share the joys and the burdens with him. I would strongly encourage you to look to the church in which God has placed you for the primary fellowship and support you need; otherwise your illusions, and the illusions of your people concern - ing you, will be fed and you will deny the reality of the Body of Christ.

> *So Elijah went from there and found Elisha son of Shaphat. He was plowing with twelve yoke of oxen, and he himself was driving the twelfth pair. Elijah went up to him and threw his cloak around him. Elisha then left his oxen and ran after Elijah. "Let me kiss my father and mother good-by," he said, "and then I will come with you." "Go back," Elijah replied. "What have I done to you?" (1 Kings 19:19,20)*

We see in Elisha a wholehearted response to God's call. He not only said good-bye to his family, but he slaughtered the oxen with which he was plowing and burned the equipment he was using.

> *So Elisha left him and went back. He took his yoke of oxen and slaughtered them. He burned the plowing equipment to cook the meat and gave it to the people, and they ate. Then he set out to follow Elijah and became his attendant. (1 Kings 19:21)*

Talk about burning your bridges behind you in light of God's call to the ministry! Elisha left nothing to which he might return. His heart was wholly turned to the work of being Elijah's servant and to the preparation for a powerful ministry as a prophet of God. I remember the way in which my co-worker Gary Olson and his wife sold their home to attend Moody Bible Institute when God called them to the ministry. They, too, have been used powerfully by God after "burning their bridges" behind them.

## GOD'S GRACIOUS PROVISIONS

We see in God's ministry to His hurting prophet Elijah many wonderful and applicable truths that will help us greatly in our own battles against spiritual, physical, or emotional *burnout*.

### God provided sleep for Elijah when he was exhausted

We, too, must be careful to receive God's provisions of rest. Many of us are not disciplined about days off, vacation times, quiet walks with our marriage partners, or the discipline of exercise.

### God provided food and water

Our Father cares about our most basic needs. Many of us get into trouble when we do not receive these gifts from His hand. Sometimes we become careless in our diets, not eating enough of the right foods or too much of the wrong ones. If we are struggling with exhaustion, a diet or even a physical exam may be a good place to start. Perhaps financial pressures have in part led to a vulnerability of losing heart. God cares about our day-to-day needs, and sharing these with our leaders may be necessary.

### God provided shelter for His prophet

God gave Elijah a place of rest and shelter over him in that process. Alongside the physical shelters that God provides for us, He gives us the shelters of His love, His people and our spiritual leaders.

### God asked the hard questions

When God confronted Elijah with the question, "What are you doing here?", He was calling His prophet to face the realities of his life and ministry. Elijah had lost his "sense of compass," his sense of direction and proportion. He had lost a sense of the sovereignty of God and his proper place in God's purposes. We, too, need to be confronted with the realities of our ministry circumstances, our choices, our attitudes, our motives, and the fruit of our work.

## God provided a ministry partner

When God gave Elisha to Elijah, He gave him the gift of someone to share the burdens and the joys of the ministry. If we see ourselves as sufficient alone to meet the needs of God's people and to defend His name, we are in a very vulnerable place.

## GO STAND IN MY PRESENCE!

If we are in trouble in the ministry, facing deep frustration, exhaustion, depression, failed expectations of ourselves or others, what do we need above all else? If we are seeking to reach out to hurting brothers or sisters who are losing heart in the ministry, what do we say to them? Do we say, "You need more rest; take some time off. You need a vacation! Get more exercise; be more careful about your diet. Find someone to whom you can be accountable. Ask for a raise."? These are all helpful, but if that is the heart of our response to hurting brothers and sisters, we will not be meeting their deepest needs or pointing them to the only place for healing and restoration.

> The LORD said, "Go out and stand on the mountain in the presence of the LORD, for the LORD is about to pass by." Then a great and powerful wind tore the mountains apart and shattered the rocks before the LORD, but the LORD was not in the wind. After the wind there was an earthquake, but the LORD was not in the earthquake. (1 Kings 19:11)

God not only met Elijah's most basic physical and emotional needs; He called Elijah into His presence. God Himself "passed by"

His prophet; He came to Elijah when his heart was hurting more than he could bear. God did not come in the bigness of the physical forces such as the power of the wind or the monumental movement of the earthquake or even the purifying, consuming heat of the fire. God came in a gentle, quiet whisper.

> *After the earthquake came a fire, but the LORD was not in the fire. And after the fire came a gentle whisper. When Elijah heard it, he pulled his cloak over his face and went out and stood at the mouth of the cave. Then a voice said to him, "What are you doing here, Elijah?" (1 Kings 19:12,13)*

When God's gentle whisper came, Elijah pulled his cloak over his face. He knew that God was there and that he was standing in the presence of the Holy One, the God who was the source of his call, his ministry and his life. What Elijah needed even more than the rest, the food and water, the shelter and the co-worker, was God. He needed God to come to him to stand in His presence.

When we are struggling with *burnout* and when our brothers and sisters are losing heart, we need God to come to us and we need to stand in His presence. We might want to say, "But that hardly sounds very practical at all! Am I really giving my brother what he needs? It seems so mystical! How do I do that? How does someone stand in His presence?"

Even as I write this, my heart is going out to a dear brother, my oldest friend, who is in the midst of overwhelming pain and pressure in the ministry. He is a faithful pastor and a wonderful teacher of the Scriptures. His church has not grown; his people are so busy and tend to be inwardly focused. They do not seem to have a heart for the lost or a vision to be the people in the community that God has called them to be. The elders have placed the responsibility on my friend and have "turned up the heat," increas - ing the pressure on Him to produce. He cannot bear this. He is not sufficient to meet their expectations. Apart from God's intervention, he will die in this situation and lose heart in the ministry.

What do I say to him? My first response is to advise, "Seek the Lord." However, the very nature of ministry *burnout* may be that our strength and desire to seek the Lord are gone, and the respon - sibility of "one more thing to do" is more than we can handle. The reminder that "then it really is up to me" is one more guilt producer for someone who is already hurting.

Because of the way God came to Elijah and through a friend's strong ministry of encouragement to me, I believe I can tell my friend that God understands where he is right now. God knows how he feels, and He cares. He has met his needs during this time just as God provided for Elijah through the widow, and He will continue to do that. I can remind him, too, that if he does not have either the strength or desire to seek God out, God will seek him out, just as He did Elijah. God will find him in his cave and get his attention, as God did with Elijah through the earthquake, the wind and the fire.

I can tell him to watch, to listen for God, and to respond as he can. When God gets his attention, He will gently whisper; then my friend will be wooed by that "Gentle Whisperer" to move out of his darkness and into God's presence. He will be able to listen and move as God enables. As he stands in His presence, God will lead him through the process of understanding how depression and *burnout* occurred. He will show him what he must do to get beyond that point. ("What are you doing here, Elijah?")

We are vulnerable to seeing the basic meeting of Elijah's needs (food, water, rest, etc.) as practical and the "standing in God's presence" as mystical. However, I do not believe that in God's sight there was a difference between the practical and the mystical. Rather, He saw an entire sphere of ministry to Elijah in which his heart could be healed and his ministry restored. So it will be for you and me. We need to receive all that God gives if we are to be sustained.

We have all been in places in which we know we should be seeking God, and yet we felt guilty for not making the effort. Satan has beaten up each of us for not "trying harder" to get close to God. But each time we are distanced from God, He has had to come and get us. It is God's movement toward us that brings us together again. He initiates wholeness and healing, and we respond as He enables us. He does this through the ministry of the Holy Spirit, who is God the Counselor and the Comforter living within us, and present with us in all of our personal and ministry circumstances.

We learn from our study of Elijah that God is committed to those He calls to ministry and that He will pursue us and give us all we need to be sustained in the work He has entrusted to us. But we not only learn that God comes to us when we are alone and hurting, we see how He comes. When we are hiding in our caves as Elijah was, what do we need? Do we need to experience a wind so powerful it will shatter us like rock? Do we need to be shaken by an earthquake, or consumed by a fire? No, we need the gentle whisper of our heavenly Father calling us into His presence.

God still speaks to us the words of life that He spoke to the Psalmist and to Elijah in that cave.

*Be still, and know that I am God; I will be exalted among the nations, I will be exalted in the earth. (Psalms 46:10)*

Only His presence will be sufficient to keep the heart of my dear friend. Likewise, nothing less than God's coming to you and to me will keep our hearts in whatever we are facing this very day. May God be gracious to us. May He come to us like He came to Elijah with all the gifts of His love and grace. May He call us into His presence where we will find the shelter for our hearts that will sustain us in the work that He has set before us!

## REFLECTIONS, COMMITMENTS AND PRAYER

*Father, thank You for the reminder that You come to Your servants who are hurting and that You will give me everything I need in every way to do all that You have entrusted to me. Thank You for providing for my most basic needs in the gifts of Your love, from the food that I eat, to the rest that refreshes me, to Your presence that sustains me. Would You protect me from a sense of myself and my work that is out of proportion and enable me to reach out to those whom You have provided to strengthen me along the way? Please teach me to watch and listen, to be sensitive when You come to me, and to respond to Your gentle whispers as You woo me to Yourself.*

*Then Moses said to him, "If your Presence does not go with us, do not send us up from here."*

*Exodus 33:15*

# 2

## *Moses:*
## *When We Are Inadequate,*
## *God Sustains Us*

**M**oses was already burned out when God found him. He had grown up in the king's household as a result of God's sovereign protection when Pharaoh sought to kill all of the male Israelite children. Then Moses had angrily killed an Egyptian and was now a shepherd hiding in the wilderness. Moses was eighty years old, a failure in this world, and the man whom God was raising up as the deliverer of His people.

I have always been amazed to see who God uses in ministry. He can use a murderer like Moses, an adulterer like David, a traitor like Peter, and one who sought to destroy His Church, Saul of Tarsus. God uses broken people to fulfill His will and to build His eternal kingdom. God has never chosen people because of who they were or what He would be able to do with them. Rather, He remains the only explanation for the fulfillment of His purposes, and He uses those who will bring Him the most glory.

Moses was used by God as the deliverer, the law-giver and the shepherd of His people. As we study Moses' life and ministry, we are reminded of God's sufficiency for weak servants and His supreme commitment to His own glory. We learn strategies for team ministry that will protect us from *burnout* and satisfy our people. We see, too, that God's presence is in fact able to sustain us when we can go no further.

Four hundred years had passed since Joseph brought his family to Egypt. The Israelites had now grown to such a great number that the Egyptians lived in fear of them. The groaning of Israel's children and the cries of their hearts went up to God.

> *God heard their groaning and he remembered his covenant with Abraham, with Isaac and with Jacob. So God looked on the Israelites and was concerned about them. (Exodus 2:24,25)*

## GOD WAS IN THE BUSH

One day in the desert near Mt. Horeb when Moses was tending sheep for his father-in-law, he suddenly became aware of a most amazing sight. A nearby bush was ablaze, and yet it did not burn up. When Moses went over to look at the bush, God spoke to him.

> *When the LORD saw that he had gone over to look, God called to him from within the bush, "Moses! Moses!" And Moses said, "Here I am." (Exodus 3:4)*

God warned Moses not to come any closer to the bush. This was holy ground, for God was present in the bush. Here we see one of the simplest, most powerful pictures in all of God's Word concerning His protection for us against burning out. Just as the bush was not consumed because God was in the bush, so we will not be consumed in ministry because of God's presence in us and around us. Then God revealed Himself to Moses as the God of his fathers.

*Then he said, "I am the God of your father, the God of Abraham, the God of Isaac and the God of Jacob." At this, Moses hid his face, because he was afraid to look at God. (Exodus 3:6)*

The compassion that filled God's heart toward His enslaved people moved Him to rescue them from the hands of their oppressors and to bring them into a land that flowed with milk and honey. Moses was God's chosen vessel, the one who would be the deliverer of His people.

*"So now, go. I am sending you to Pharaoh to bring my people the Israelites out of Egypt." (Exodus 3:10)*

How did Moses respond? Did he fall on his face with thanksgiving for God's heart of compassion toward His captive, hurting people? Did he worship this God who was calling him to be His servant? No, there is no thanksgiving or worship seen in Moses' heart. In fact, there is no turning toward the God of his fathers who reigns in holiness and power. Moses' focus immediately turned inward. "Why me?"

*But Moses said to God, "Who am I, that I should go to Pharaoh and bring the Israelites out of Egypt?" (Exodus 3:11)*

Moses demonstrated no heart for God and no commitment to His people. There appears to be no desire to be involved with God or what He is doing. We know from studying the following Scriptures that Moses was consumed with his own weakness, inadequacy and fear. But God reveals the one thing that will make all of the difference in the world for Moses and for you and me. For those who are self-focused, confronted with their own overwhelming lack of ability, there is only one answer: God is there.

*And God said, "I will be with you. And this will be the sign to you that it is I who have sent you: When you have brought the people*

> *out of Egypt, you will worship God on this mountain."*
> *(Exodus 3:12)*

## I WILL BE WITH YOU

It was the promise of God's presence that should have set Moses' heart free. By everything he had known and heard of God, he should have been immediately filled with confidence. But he was unmoved. Moses, the greatest of Old Testament saints, responded just as we probably would. The enemy was right there filling his mind and heart with a myriad of "what if" questions and speculations.

> *Moses said to God, "Suppose I go to the Israelites and say to them, 'The God of your fathers has sent me to you,' and they ask me, 'What is his name?' Then what shall I tell them?"*
> *(Exodus 3:13)*

Once again God is the only answer provided for Moses. The God who would be with him is the ever-present, ever-living, all-sufficient God. How often do we remain consumed with our own weaknesses and inadequacies, even in the light of all that we know about God? For us, too, the promise of His presence and the sufficiency of His power flowing out of His eternal Name are all that God provides for us in the midst of His call on our lives.

> *God said to Moses, "I AM WHO I AM. This is what you are to say to the Israelites: 'I AM has sent me to you.'" (Exodus 3:14)*

God instructed Moses to gather the elders of His people together and reveal that God had appeared to him with the promise of His deliverance. He warned Moses that Pharaoh would not let them go but that God would display His power and that the Egyptians would give them the wealth of the land. However, Moses remained unconvinced!

*Moses answered, "What if they do not believe me or listen to me and say, 'The LORD did not appear to you'?" (Exodus 4:1)*

Again the enemy filled Moses' heart with the "what if" questions. Although God demonstrated His power by turning Moses' staff into a snake, by turning his hand leprous and then healing him, and by assuring Moses that there would be many other miraculous signs before His people as well as the Egyptians, Moses' argumentative spirit was not yet broken.

*Moses said to the LORD, "O Lord, I have never been eloquent, neither in the past nor since you have spoken to your servant. I am slow of speech and tongue." (Exodus 4:10)*

## I HAVE NEVER BEEN ELOQUENT

Moses brought all of his best excuses before the Lord. He knew that God could not use him because he was not a very good speaker. Surely God would need someone of eloquence to represent Him before Pharaoh and His people. How we worship eloquence! Though disproportionally we place importance on the gifts of teaching and preaching, God reminded Moses that He knew all about his weakness; in fact, He is sovereign over physical limitations.

*The LORD said to him, "Who gave man his mouth? Who makes him deaf or mute? Who gives him sight or makes him blind? Is it not I, the LORD?" (Exodus 4:11)*

Now Moses blatantly bails out of God's call! The truth is that he is not only consumed with his weaknesses and inadequacies, he really wants nothing more to do with God or His people. Surely, the fear of man is a major struggle for Moses as he would need to stand before his enemy, Pharaoh.

> *"Now go; I will help you speak and will teach you what to say."*
> *But Moses said, "O Lord, please send someone else to do it."*
> *(Exodus 4:12,13)*

With this last-ditch evasion, Moses finally crossed the line. God's anger burned against Moses. God wanted to enrich Moses' life and use him for His own glory and for Moses' own good, but Moses couldn't see it. God became angry with his stubborn unbelief. Moses was so inwardly focused that he kept missing the heart of God's call and the assurance of His presence. "I will be with you...I will help you speak...I will teach you what to say...I will teach you what to do." What confidence is ours in this great truth!

The same God who was the source of Moses' call, who promised to be sufficient for all that He set before him, and who assured him of His presence is the God who is sufficient for you and me. Where in the ministry have you felt inadequate? Where has your sense of unworthiness caused you to hide? When have you felt God's keeping presence sustain you in your weakness? The God of Moses is the same God who has called you and me, and He will sustain us as well.

## WHO IS THE LORD?

Moses not only confronted his own inadequacies and lack of heart in the ministry, he also faced a very formidable foe. Pharaoh had a good thing going with the free labor that came from hundreds of thousands of enslaved Israelites. He was not about to lose their valuable contribution to his kingdom and also lose face in the process. When Moses and Aaron went to Pharaoh with God's message, "Let my people go," Pharaoh responded with all of the pride that came with his earthly power and position.

*Pharaoh said, "Who is the LORD, that I should obey him and let Israel go? I do not know the LORD and I will not let Israel go." (Exodus 5:2)*

Without knowing it, Pharaoh was asking the key question of this entire experience, for himself and for Israel: "Who is the Lord?" God's purposes for His enslaved children, for His inadequate leader, and for this pride-filled monarch were all being orchestrated now to answer that very question. God had designed these circumstances over centuries, to reveal before all who were watching that He is the sovereign One.

Rather than releasing Israel to worship God, Pharaoh commanded them to work even harder, to gather their own straw to make bricks. God's people were under great pressure, and the workload was more than they could bear. Pharaoh accused them of laziness, and the people complained to Moses who, in turn, complained to the Lord.

*Moses returned to the LORD and said, "O Lord, why have you brought trouble upon this people? Is this why you sent me? Ever since I went to Pharaoh to speak in your name, he has brought trouble upon this people, and you have not rescued your people at all." (Exodus 5:22,23)*

God is putting Himself on display in this situation, but Moses is not able to catch the significance of what is taking place. Moses still thinks the whole event centers around the deliverance of Israel, but he is wrong. This situation centers around who God is and what He will do to display His power and His glory in order that all the earth might worship Him. The apostle Paul reveals that great truth in his letter to the Romans.

*For the Scripture says to Pharaoh: "I raised you up for this very purpose, that I might display my power in you and that my name might be proclaimed in all the earth." (Romans 9:17)*

## GOD ON DISPLAY

It is also crucial for us to remember that the circumstances and situations that we, our people and our missions face are being designed by God to put Himself on display. Beyond the projects, the outreaches, the services, the relationships and the circumstances, lie God's great, eternal purposes of displaying His power and His glory through us. That is usually seen in our responses to what is happening and in our relationships in the process, rather than the goals and objectives we are accomplishing.

God now tells Moses what He will do.

> *Then the LORD said to Moses, "Now you will see what I will do to Pharaoh: Because of my mighty hand he will let them go; because of my mighty hand he will drive them out of his country."*
> *(Exodus 6:1)*

Moses needed to be reminded again that the purpose in all of this is who God is and what He will do to reveal His great power! As God prepares Moses further for the ministry He has set before him, we see a wonderful picture in verses 2-8 of Exodus 6. While Moses has been consumed with what he is unable to do, he needed to listen to what God would do! "I am the Lord. I appeared to Abraham...I established my covenant...I have heard the groanings of the Israelites...I have remembered my covenant...I am the Lord, and I will bring you out...I will free you...I will redeem you...I will take you as my own people and I will be your God. Then you will know that I am the Lord. I will bring you to the land...I will give it to you as a possession. I am the Lord."

What weakness that we bear could immobilize us before a God of such great sufficiency? How often do we see our own lack of eloquence or lack of strength or lack of boldness or lack of knowledge and maturity as a barrier in ministry? When our focus becomes turned inward upon ourselves and we see only what we lack, our enemy paralyzes us. We, too, must focus on our great, sufficient God and all that He will do.

Yet, when Moses reported to the Israelites all that God had said to him, they remained unmoved.

> *Moses reported this to the Israelites, but they did not listen to him because of their discouragement and cruel bondage.*
> *(Exodus 6:9)*

God remained firm in His call. "Go tell Pharaoh to let my people go!" But Moses had no more confidence than before.

> *But Moses said to the LORD, "If the Israelites will not listen to me, why would Pharaoh listen to me, since I speak with faltering lips?" (Exodus 6:12)*

## GOD WILL GAIN GLORY FOR HIMSELF

We are reminded again that God does not call people because of who they are or what He will be able to do through them. God, His sovereign choices and His glory are the only basis of His call in our lives. We see, too, that regardless of the resistance from political systems, the forces of darkness, or leaders who do not want to follow, God will fulfill the purposes of His heart in the precise ways that please Him the most.

We see in the unfolding of the ten plagues the agonizing process of God's will being worked out. The pain, the loss of life, the darkness and the turning back and forth of Pharaoh's heart exhaust us, and we are just reading the account! After the last plague, when every first born was killed and the Passover established, God tells us the point of it all. Now we know why His process is the way it is.

> *And I will harden Pharaoh's heart, and he will pursue them. But I will gain glory for myself through Pharaoh and all his army, and the Egyptians will know that I am the LORD. (Exodus 14:4a)*

God is preparing the way of escape for Israel and the way of destruction for His enemies. His battle strategy, however, centers around His eternal purposes rather than temporal deliverance. God has designed this entire process in order to gain the most glory for Himself!

> *"I will harden the hearts of the Egyptians so that they will go in after them. And I will gain glory through Pharaoh and all his army, through his chariots and his horsemen. The Egyptians will know that I am the LORD when I gain glory through Pharaoh, his chariots and his horsemen." (Exodus 14:17,18)*

God hardened the hearts of Pharaoh and the Egyptians and opened the Red Sea for His people in order to gain glory for Himself. God delights in gaining glory at the expense of His enemies and through the obedience of His people.

In whatever circumstances we find ourselves in ministry, we cannot afford to get caught up only in the immediate situations, the pressing needs, the incredible opportunities, the pain-filled relationships, or even the call of God for a particular work. We must keep the larger picture in view. Just as God's purposes for Moses were higher than being His deliverer for His enslaved people, so God's purposes for you and me are higher than the work at which we labor with all of our hearts every day. God is designing our circumstances, our relationships, and our ministries in such a way that He will gain the most glory for Himself. Although His commitment to His own glory sometimes costs us dearly because this is God's great goal, it must become ours as well.

## YOU ARE GOING TO WEAR OUT!

It was not only his own sin and inadequacies that caused Moses to battle *burnout*, nor was it an overwhelming enemy in Pharaoh, but after crossing the Red Sea Moses carried a workload that threatened to destroy him.

*The next day Moses took his seat to serve as judge for the people, and they stood around him from morning till evening. (Exodus 18:13)*

Moses was the deliverer, the leader, and the judge of God's people. From morning until evening they came with their problems. God gave a gift to Moses at this time through the discernment of his father-in-law.

*When his father-in-law saw all that Moses was doing for the people, he said, "What is this you are doing for the people? Why do you alone sit as judge, while all these people stand around you from morning till evening?" (Exodus 18:14)*

It is clear that Moses bought into this incredible workload and carried the burden of being the "wisdom source" for God's people.

*Moses answered him, "Because the people come to me to seek God's will. Whenever they have a dispute, it is brought to me, and I decide between the parties and inform them of God's decrees and laws." (Exodus 18:15,16)*

God used Jethro to confront Moses with the reality of his situation, for he would wear out if he continued to take all of the responsibility for the people upon himself.

*Moses' father-in-law replied, "What you are doing is not good. You and these people who come to you will only wear yourselves out. The work is too heavy for you; you cannot handle it alone." (Exodus 18:17,18)*

Jethro, used by God as a protection for Moses, wisely laid out for him a ministry plan built around a team concept.

*"Listen now to me and I will give you some advice, and may God be with you. You must be the people's representative before God and bring their disputes to him. Teach them the decrees and laws,*

*and show them the way to live and the duties they are to per-form." (Exodus 18:19,20)*

The plan is for Moses to do what he is gifted and called to do and seek other team members to help him by sharing the load of ministry and supporting him in the process.

*"But select capable men from all the people—men who fear God, trustworthy men who hate dishonest gain—and appoint them as officials over thousands, hundreds, fifties and tens. Have them serve as judges for the people at all times, but have them bring every difficult case to you; the simple cases they can decide them-selves. That will make your load lighter, because they will share it with you." (Exodus 18:21,22)*

In this way Moses could more effectively handle the demands of the ministry, and the needs of the people would be met more fully. It is important to note that Jethro encouraged Moses to se-lect "capable men." Often, because of church politics or the pres-sure to fill slots, we put people into office who do not have the spiritual qualifications. The pressure and pain that result from this short-range vision have produced *burnout* in many pastors.

*"If you do this and God so commands, you will be able to stand the strain, and all these people will go home satisfied."*
*(Exodus 18:23)*

We are reminded once again of the significance of a team min-istry. None of us has all of the gifts, resources and strengths to meet the needs or the demands of the people we are serving. We, too, must seek the partnership of other gifted men and women in the work. We do not know whether Moses' view of himself as the sole source of wisdom was setting him up for *burnout* or whether he fell into this naively, but he surely needed the wisdom of Jethro to protect him. Moses expressed great vulnerability and submitted to his father-in-law. When we see ourselves as part of the Body and are submissive to leadership, God will use these attitudes to protect us. We must be continually asking God, "Who are the 'Jethros' that you have given to me?"

There is another truth revealed in Jethro's ministry that God will use to protect us from *burnout*. He told Moses that by sharing the leadership with others, he would be able to stand the strain and *the people would be satisfied* as well. No one person is able to satisfy the needs of a congregation. In the wisdom of shared leadership, God's people are satisfied, and a satisfied congregation is part of our Father's protection against His leaders' losing heart.

This is a reminder, too, of one of the most important ministries of our elders. We have come to applaud hard work, even at times to find our affirmation in the number of hours that we work. This lifestyle identifies commitment and confirms our call. Sometimes those of us in the ministry lose sight of what is happening. Wise elders will not permit their pastors or missionaries to work 60-80 hours a week endlessly with few days off. They will see it as their stewardship to protect their servants from *burnout*, even as Jethro did with Moses. This ministry may come in gentle counsel or strong confrontation, but it must be done!

## YOU WANT TO GO BACK TO EGYPT?

It wasn't just the workload that burdened Moses; it was the hard-hearted unbelief of Israel. They continually failed to see God's promises or to trust in the power of His care. When Moses sent out the spies to look at the promised land, ten came back affirming that it was a land flowing with milk and honey but filled with fear because of the giants that lived there. Rather than believing that God would once again deliver their enemies into their hands, they became paralyzed by their own weaknesses. They refused to see themselves through the eyes of God and accepted their enemy's view.

> *"We saw the Nephilim there (the descendants of Anak come from the Nephilim). We seemed like grasshoppers in our own eyes, and we looked the same to them." (Numbers 13:33)*

After hearing the report, the people whined and wept, grumbled and rebelled. They completely lost a sense of identity in God and His great purposes for them.

> *That night all the people of the community raised their voices and wept aloud. All the Israelites grumbled against Moses and Aaron, and the whole assembly said to them, "If only we had died in Egypt! Or in this desert!" (Numbers 14:1,2)*

The Israelites had quickly forgotten the pain of slavery in Egypt. They cried out against Moses and Aaron and wished they had died in the desert. They refused to believe God's promise to bring them into the land, thus a rebellion arose and they made plans to choose a leader to take them back to Egypt.

> *"Why is the LORD bringing us to this land only to let us fall by the sword? Our wives and children will be taken as plunder. Wouldn't it be better for us to go back to Egypt?" And they said to each other, "We should choose a leader and go back to Egypt." (Numbers 14:3,4)*

### REBELLION AMONG THE PEOPLE

Moses and Aaron could not believe what was happening. They prostrated themselves before God's people. Joshua and Caleb, who had assured the people that God was again able to deliver them, tore their clothes. They reminded Israel once again of God's protection and His presence.

> *"Only do not rebel against the LORD. And do not be afraid of the people of the land, because we will swallow them up. Their protection is gone, but the LORD is with us. Do not be afraid of them." (Numbers 14:9)*

The response of the children of Israel was a desire to kill their leaders! Only God's presence saved Moses, Aaron, Joshua and Caleb from death.

*But the whole assembly talked about stoning them. Then the glory of the LORD appeared at the Tent of Meeting to all the Israelites. (Numbers 14:10)*

In His anger God talked of destroying Israel at that place and raising up a new people through Moses, but Moses became more committed to God and His purposes than to any reputation he might gain. He reminded God of His covenant commitments to His people and pleaded with God to forgive His children. As a result, God's mercy was seen; He did not destroy Israel at that place, but none of those who rebelled were able to enter the promised land. They wandered in the wilderness for forty years, and they all died.

Many of our churches and our missions live in Numbers 13 and 14. As God calls His people onward, setting before us lands to possess and ministries to fulfill, so many of His people refuse to believe that God can really do it. They see themselves as grasshoppers, and become paralyzed by their smallness. God wants to set them free with His greatness, but too many of His people cannot see how big He is. They have little eyes that only see themselves and their immediate circumstances.

In these situations churches not only refuse to move on, but they live in the past, dreaming about how it used to be ("I want to go back to Egypt"). Often these churches turn on their leaders and sometimes even try to destroy them. How many churches have "wandered in the wilderness" for years, having no ministry of significance, because of a refusal to believe God or to see themselves through His eyes! Most pastors hunger for their people to be involved in outreach ministries in the community or to expand their vision for missions. They want to send out more people for short-term projects, but the church remains committed only to the "status quo," fearing for the security of their ministry at home or their finances. Sometimes the people see the pastor as the problem, as he is always talking about more outreach. How often have pastors lost heart in these situations! When the people are after us, ready to throw stones, only God can preserve us. God protected Moses and Aaron, and He will protect you and me as well.

## LET MY ANGER BURN!

Of course, the incident at Kadesh was not the first time the Israelites had lost their identity and rebelled in their sin. Three months after they left Egypt, God instructed Moses to assemble His people at Mt. Sinai where God gave Moses the Law, the character of His heart written on those tablets of stone. Moses was probably hungry for even more of God's presence after forty days on the mountain in intimate communication with his Father. Yet when he came down, he saw the people worshiping a golden calf.

> *Then the LORD said to Moses, "Go down, because your people, whom you brought up out of Egypt, have become corrupt. They have been quick to turn away from what I commanded them and have made themselves an idol cast in the shape of a calf. They have bowed down to it and sacrificed to it and have said, 'These are your gods, O Israel, who brought you up out of Egypt.'"*
> *(Exodus 32:7,8)*

God's anger was so great that He talked of destroying His people, but Moses reminded Him of His purposes and His covenant commitments. God's judgments on His people were harsh that day, and many Israelites died. God told Moses to leave that place and proceed to the land He had promised. Then God made an incredible statement:

*"I will send an angel before you and drive out the Canaanites, Amorites, Hittites, Perizzites, Hivites and Jebusites. Go up to the land flowing with milk and honey. But I will not go with you, because you are a stiff-necked people and I might destroy you on the way."* *(Exodus 33:2,3)*

Now this is an unbelievable situation. God appears to be "burned out"! How do we deal with this? God will not go any further with His people; He will send an angel to go with them. The people begin to mourn and weep when they hear these distressing words.

*For the LORD had said to Moses, "Tell the Israelites, 'You are a stiff-necked people. If I were to go with you even for a moment, I might destroy you. Now take off your ornaments and I will decide what to do with you.'"* *(Exodus 33:5)*

We find then the description of the Tent of Meeting where Moses would go to meet with God. The presence of God, the pillar of cloud, would stand at the entrance to the Tent, and all the people would worship. The expression of intimacy between God and Moses recorded in the Scriptures makes us hunger for God's presence as well.

*The LORD would speak to Moses face to face, as a man speaks with his friend. Then Moses would return to the camp, but his young aide Joshua son of Nun did not leave the tent.* *(Exodus 33:11)*

## WITHOUT YOUR PRESENCE, I CANNOT GO ON

Moses now confronted God with the reality of his situation. Not only was he keenly aware of his inadequacy, but now he felt alone as well and could not bear it nor could he go on. He hungered more and more to know God.

> *Moses said to the LORD, "You have been telling me, 'Lead these people,' but you have not let me know whom you will send with me. You have said, 'I know you by name and you have found favor with me.' If you are pleased with me, teach me your ways so I may know you and continue to find favor with you. Remember that this nation is your people." (Exodus 33:12,13)*

God knew that Moses needed the reality of His presence and the assurance that He would go with him from that place. God spoke the words that Moses needed to hear.

> *The LORD replied, "My Presence will go with you, and I will give you rest." (Exodus 33:14)*

It was as though Moses did not hear God. His heart was still filled with the fear that God might abandon him and His people.

> *Then Moses said to him, "If your Presence does not go with us, do not send us up from here. How will anyone know that you are pleased with me and with your people unless you go with us? What else will distinguish me and your people from all the other people on the face of the earth?" (Exodus 33:15,16)*

Moses could not go on without God's sustaining presence which would be able to keep him and the children of Israel. Only His presence would distinguish them from all the peoples of the world.

This truth transforms churches and missions. God's presence is not only His keeping grace for our hearts, but it is our distinguishing mark. When people come into our churches or have contact with our ministries, in the final analysis it is not our programs, our songs, our sermons or our dreams that will captivate them. Only when they sense "God is here!" will they realize that we are different from the world around us. People are able to sense the reality of God in our worship, our unity, our love for one another, our serving and our giving. It is God's presence that we must seek above all else if we would have an impact of lasting significance.

## A PLACE TO STAND

Now God says something to Moses that each one of us would love to hear.

*And the LORD said to Moses, "I will do the very thing you have asked, because I am pleased with you and I know you by name." (Exodus 33:17)*

For God to be pleased with us and to have a relationship of intimacy with us would fulfill us more than any organizational goal we could accomplish! Moses brought to God the boldest request in history.

*Then Moses said, "Now show me your glory." (Exodus 33:18)*

Although Moses hungered to see God's face, God revealed His heart to him. Who He is, what He is like, the way in which He gives Himself to people is what God showed to His servant. He proclaimed His Name and He revealed His mercy, but Moses would be consumed if He saw the fullness of God's holiness and glory.

*And the LORD said, "I will cause all my goodness to pass in front of you, and I will proclaim my name, the LORD, in your presence. I will have mercy on whom I will have mercy, and I will have compassion on whom I will have compassion. But," he said, "you cannot see my face, for no one may see me and live." (Exodus 33:19,20)*

God graciously met Moses at the place of his heart's request. God put him in the cleft of the rock, covered him with His hand, and as He passed by, Moses saw His glory. Though Moses hungered to see God's face, God revealed to him the glory of His heart.

God's presence provided a sanctuary for Moses in which he was healed and enabled to continue in the ministry of leading His people. Just as we saw with Elijah, God came to Moses when he was hurting and provided for him in his time of need.

> *Then the Lord said, "There is a place near me where you may stand on a rock. When my glory passes by, I will put you in a cleft in the rock and cover you with my hand until I have passed by."* *(Exodus 33:21,22)*

Can you imagine any more encouraging words for a hurting shepherd to hear? Moses was at the end of his own resources, he had lost heart, and he had no hope of continuing in the ministry apart from God's presence. If God had not met him here, Moses would have sunk under the waves of despair. But the One who had called him was there in His everlasting faithfulness to say: "There is a place near Me where you may stand on a rock, and the glory of My presence will meet you there!" That is our heavenly Father's promise to you and me as well when we are losing heart, feeling empty or sinking in despair. There is a place near Him where we can stand on a rock. On that firm foundation, His glorious presence will meet us and become our sustaining grace.

Moses had communed with God for forty days. God had given him the Law. Without question this was the highest point of Moses' life and ministry. Then he was confronted with the reality of a depraved and disobedient people, and he lost heart. He destroyed the tablets of stone. Only God's glorious presence was able to sustain him.

## A Sense of His Presence

It is God's presence that keeps us even when we are exhausted in situations that would seem to overwhelm us. There is a physicalness about His presence that transforms us and sets us free. On a recent trip to the Philippines, I was confronted with my need for the reality of God's presence in my life. I left my Chicago home early in the morning, and after a 24-hour trip during which I crossed the international date line and with hardly any sleep on the airplanes, I arrived at my destination in Manila the next day. I was already depressed because of leaving my wife, my family and all the things I enjoy about the comforts of home, but I had a day to visit with my hosts and rest.

Then the ministry began in earnest! From 9:00 a.m. to 4:00 p.m. the next day I taught a complete seminar. Then I traveled to another church a few hours outside of Manila and taught another all-day seminar. The heat and the relentless mosquitoes were complicating my situation, and I was waking up between 3:00 - 4:00 each morning because my time zones were almost completely reversed. The next day I returned to Manila and spoke to a group of pastors during a luncheon meeting and began another seminar in a local church that evening.

During the next two days I was scheduled to teach in yet another church, but my heart was lifted when I heard that I would be staying in a hotel for those nights. At last, I could have some quietness and air conditioning and hot showers! During those two days I could get caught up on my rest and be able to get a boost for the heavy schedule to follow in the next couple of weeks. Afterwards I was scheduled to fly to Bacolod where I would spend the weekend with a group of people whom I loved dearly and minister at their church. Just as I was beginning to enjoy the cool restfulness of the hotel, my friend Ernie called me from Bacolod and told me that I would have to change my flight because the one I was booked on was not operating due to an airline dispute. When I proceeded to change my flight with Philippine Airlines, I was assured that there was no need to change since the flight was operating.

I was thankful for a good night's sleep, but the next day, still unsure about the flight situation, I went to another Philippine Airlines office to check on the flight. I was told, "They wouldn't have sold you a ticket if the flight was not operating!" Somewhat more assured, I prepared for that evening's seminar. At about 10:00 p.m., just as we were preparing to leave the church building, I received a call from Ernie in Bacolod. "They lied to you, Bill. That flight has not been operating all week!"

By that time, all of the other direct flights to Bacolod were filled, and the only way I could get there the next day was to fly to a neighboring island and take a ferry. That meant I would have to take the 3:00 a.m. flight in order to catch the 7:00 a.m. ferry. All I could do was get an hour's sleep, pack and leave for the airport at 1:30 a.m. After the flight, I took a taxi to the ferry and was able to get on early. As I sat in my seat trying to get some rest, I was exhausted, frustrated and angry, and sleep would not come.

## TRANSFORMED IN HIS PRESENCE

The ferry left the dock at 7:00 a.m. Still unable to sleep, I decided to leave the air conditioned area with the large comfortable seats and sit on one of the deck chairs outside. The sun was just coming up over the beautiful islands of the Philippines. I took my Bible and began to read several of the Psalms in which David speaks of God as his fortress, his refuge and his deliverer. God began to speak to my heart, softening my anger and strengthening me in my tiredness. He began to give me an awareness of His presence and surrounded me with a sense of His love and care. The reality of His presence was so great that it was as if God had come and physically sat in the chair next to me on that ship! Before long I was not grumbling; I was singing! Rather than complaining, I was thanking God for His goodness to me. God's presence had filled my heart with His peace.

One of the books I had taken with me on this trip was *Shadow of the Almighty* by Elisabeth Elliot. In this book, through letters and diary excerpts, she tells the story of her husband Jim who was martyred by the Auca Indians in Ecuador. About this time on the trip I had just read the following excerpts from Jim's diary in 1951. He was 23 years old and working as a salesman while he was preparing for God to take him to Ecuador. He was also developing radio programs to communicate God's heart for missions. On January 15, 1951, he wrote the following:

> *January 15. "There is that restlessness, that itching, urging discontent in me this morning. The milk of the Word curdles before me or seems to sour within. Hatefulness and rebellion against all restraint is not far from the surface; and it is good that I am not alone here. 'Lead me not into temptation, but deliver me from evil.'"[1]*

One of the things I greatly appreciated about Jim Elliot's diary was his humanness and his willingness to be honest about himself. He was not afraid to be vulnerable, to be known. On the next day, January 16, 1951, he wrote the following:

> *January 16. "Feel that I must write something tonight in praise of the God of delights. The day passed slowly with little affairs; two conferences for Hytool sales, contract signing for a radio program, some poor script writing, all with a sense of waiting on God for His time, His H-Hour. All day the sun dropped hints of spring, and at dusk, returning from the shop I exulted in the distinct wall of purple—the Ozark foothills—close-guarded by the unblinking Venus. The night*

1 Elisabeth Elliot, *Shadow of the Almighty*, Harper & Row, San Francisco, 1956, pp. 141-2.

*spread black and blossomed brilliantly with stars. I walked out to the hill just now. It is exalting, delicious. To stand embraced by the shadows of a friendly tree with the wind tugging at your coattails and the heavens hailing your heart—to gaze and glory and to give oneself again to God, what more could a man ask? Oh the fullness, pleasure, sheer excitement of knowing God on earth. I care not if I ever raise my voice again for Him, if only I may love Him, please Him. Mayhap in mercy He shall give me a host of children that I may lead through the vast star fields, to explore His delicacies, whose finger-ends set them to burning. But if not, if only I may see Him, touch His garments, and smile into my Lover's eyes—ah, then, not stars, nor children shall matter—only Himself.*"[2]

How I hunger to live with a sense of God's presence like that! "Oh the fullness, pleasure, sheer excitement of knowing God on earth!" We, like Jim Elliot, are transformed when we sense God's presence. My difficulties during those days in the Philippines were surely nothing compared to what Moses experienced with the children of Israel, but God's presence was real to me in my time of need; He sustained my heart.

Perhaps you are in circumstances right now that are overwhelming your heart. Perhaps your people are not following your leading, or even turning against you. Maybe they want to return to the "good old days" in Egypt, and you are weary of continually reminding them of God's power and sufficiency when they refuse to listen. It could even be that you have said, "If you do not go with me, God, I cannot go on from here. I need your presence to surround me and my people! I need you to give me rest!" God will meet you there with the resources of His Holy Spirit, and His

---

2 *Shadow of the Almighty*, p. 142

presence will sustain you. Ask to see His face, and God will show you His heart. His Name will remind you that you belong to Him, and His compassion will carry you.

### REFLECTIONS, COMMITMENTS AND PRAYER

*God, would You enable me to see all that You will do in the midst of all that I cannot do? Would You remind me day after day that the great "I Am" is the One who fills me, even as You filled that bush before Moses' eyes? Lord, teach me to reach out to other team members that You have given to me and even to be submissive to their counsel. God, give me a hunger to seek Your face! Please surround me with Your glorious presence, which alone can sustain me when nothing seems to be going according to plan.*

*One thing I ask of the LORD, this is what I seek: that I may dwell in the house of the LORD all the days of my life, to gaze upon the beauty of the LORD and to seek him in his temple.*

*Psalms 27:4*

# 3

## *David:*
## *When We Are Thirsty,*
## *God Satisfies Us*

Whether we read about the great men and women of the Scrip-tures, it is not so much their courage or even the power of their exploits that grips us. Rather, the intimacy with which they walked with God stirs within us a passion to know Him as they knew Him. We read about the apostle Paul, hear of his great afflictions, and see how God used him in the building of His Church, and our hearts are moved. When he says, "For to me, to live is Christ" (Phil. 1:21), our hearts want to be drawn far beyond what we have experienced with Jesus. Later in the same letter he says the following:

*I want to know Christ and the power of his resurrection and the fellowship of sharing in his sufferings, becoming like him in his death, and so, somehow, to attain to the resurrection from the dead. (Philippians 3:10,11)*

There is inflamed passion here which awakens and focuses our own desires. Perhaps there is a hint of jealousy in our hearts when we read of what Enoch experienced when he "walked with God; then he was no more, because God took him away" (Gen. 5:24). When we see that Abraham was called God's friend (2 Chron. 20:7) and that God knew Moses by name (Ex. 33:17), we hunger for that same intimacy and fullness of life with our Father in heaven. However, when God calls David a man "after His own heart" (1 Sam 13:14) we cry out, "I, too, want that kind of relationship with God!"

## A Heart after God

David is one of the great enigmas of the Scriptures. In him we see a great depth of failure and sin, yet a heart that passionately pursues God. The Bible graphically describes his adultery with Bathsheba and then the murder of her husband Uriah when David sought to cover her pregnancy and his sin. We see the weakness of his kingdom and the breakdown of his family. That he could be a man after God's own heart finds its explanation only in our Father's deep and mysterious mercies. It also encourages each one of us who passionately desires to know God.

Because God wants us to learn from David's example, He calls David "a witness to the peoples" (Isa. 55:3,4). David's passionate love for God and the responsiveness of his heart before the Lord teach us about the necessity of stirring the inner core of our relationship with God. David's life and the enduring ministry of his Psalms testify that all we are flows primarily out of our passions. The enflamed affections of our souls focused Godward are our most basic protection from burning out in the ministry.

We can hardly imagine circumstances more designed to pro - duce *burnout* than those that David faced. Not all *burnout* is caused by sin, of course, but David's sins surely formed the framework for his own failure. Perhaps because of the way in which he modeled his own rebellious sexual lifestyle before his children, David's son Amnon felt a measure of sexual license as he raped his own half-sister Tamar. David knew about the incident and was furious, but he never mentioned it to Amnon and there were no immediate consequences. David's son Absalom loved his sister Tamar and was deeply grieved over this terrible thing that had been done to her. He waited for two years, and when his father still had not sought justice in the matter, Absalom arranged for Amnon to be killed.

After the death of Amnon, Absalom fled to Geshur and remained there three years. The Scriptures tell us that "the spirit of the king longed to go to Absalom" (2 Sam. 13:39), but he did not do it. Because Joab, David's commander, knew that the king's heart longed for Absalom, he arranged for a wise woman of Tekoa to go to David with a story which revealed God's heart for those who are estranged. When David was confronted with what he had done in banishing Absalom for killing Amnon, the woman summarized God's message in this way.

> *Like water spilled on the ground, which cannot be recovered, so we must die. But God does not take away life; instead, he devises ways so that a banished person may not remain estranged from him.. (2 Samuel 14:14)*

David was now willing to let Absalom return to Jerusalem. Joab himself went to Geshur and brought Absalom back to his father's city, but David made another terrible decision. He refused to see Absalom. His acceptance of his son was tentative and half-hearted.

> *But the king said, "He must go to his own house; he must not see my face." So Absalom went to his own house and did not see the face of the king. (2 Samuel 14:24)*

## I WANT TO SEE MY FATHER'S FACE!

For a son who had been banished for three years, this was a terrible blow. He had been grieving because of the terrible sin to his sister, and he had Amnon killed because it seemed that justice had not been done. When Absalom was allowed to return home after three years, he heard from his own father, "He must not see my face!"

Thus, Absalom lived in Jerusalem for two years without seeing the king, which meant it had been five years since he had been in his father's presence. Absalom sent for Joab twice to take him to the king, but Joab refused. In order to get his father's attention, Absalom told his servants to set Joab's barley field on fire.

> *Then Joab did go to Absalom's house and he said to him, "Why have your servants set my field on fire?" Absalom said to Joab, "Look, I sent word to you and said, 'Come here so I can send you to the king to ask, "Why have I come from Geshur? It would be better for me if I were still there!" ' Now then, I want to see the king's face, and if I am guilty of anything, let him put me to death." (2 Samuel 14:31,32)*

When children feel estranged from their fathers, they do have ways of getting their attention! In fact, children have an incredible variety of creative ways to gain their father's attention when they feel that the fathers are caught up in other things and will not give them the time, the access and the intimacy they need. In fact, many pastors who are struggling with *burnout* are being confronted with the pain and pressure of family circumstances and relationships because their children have been "setting their fields on fire."

When we hear Absalom crying out, "I want to see my father's face," our own hearts are deeply moved. How could a father continue to banish a son like this and bring such pain to his heart? David appeared to be so preoccupied with building his own great kingdom that he seemed unaware of the deep pain, anger and bitterness that was developing in his own son's heart because of a lack of relationship with his father.

We cannot be reminded too many times that we must keep our own priorities straight in the ministry. How many of us are building great kingdoms—beautiful, powerful, significant works in the eyes of many—when our own children are crying to see our faces. We need to protect their hearts from anger and bitterness, not only toward us, but toward God, by giving of ourselves to them.

> *So Joab went to the king and told him this. Then the king summoned Absalom, and he came in and bowed down with his face to the ground before the king. And the king kissed Absalom. (2 Samuel 14:33)*

Absalom had now gained not only Joab's attention, but the king's as well. David summoned his son, received him and kissed him, but it was too little, too late.

## ABSALOM MY SON, MY SON

Absalom was a very attractive man and politically astute. He began to present himself before the people of Israel as one who would really be attentive to their needs and give them the representation they desired. He was so effective in his campaign that he was able to turn the hearts of the people toward himself and away from his own father David.

> *Also, whenever anyone approached him to bow down before him, Absalom would reach out his hand, take hold of him and kiss him. (2 Samuel 15:5)*

After four years of campaigning, Absalom set himself up as king in Hebron. The hearts of the people were so attracted to Absalom that the once-powerful King David had to flee from his own son and from the powerful forces that had joined with Absalom in opposition to him. David is a broken man, humiliated by his own sins and by his own family.

> *But David continued up the Mount of Olives, weeping as he went; his head was covered and he was barefoot. All the people with him covered their heads too and were weeping as they went up.* (2 Samuel 15:30)

David was almost completely destroyed in the battles that followed. Great was his humiliation when Absalom slept with David's concubines on the roof of the palace before the eyes of the entire nation. After David's sin with Bathsheba, the prophet Nathan had told him that this would be one of the consequences to his sin. The three consequences were that the son born to them would die, the sword would never depart from his house, and his wives would be given in broad daylight to one close to him.

> *"This is what the LORD says: 'Out of your own household I am going to bring calamity upon you. Before your very eyes I will take your wives and give them to one who is close to you, and he will lie with your wives in broad daylight. You did it in secret, but I will do this thing in broad daylight before all Israel.'"* (2 Samuel 12:11,12)

Only by God's grace and the loyalty of his own troops was Absalom narrowly defeated and David's kingdom preserved. David had asked his soldiers to be careful with Absalom in the battle and to preserve his life, but Absalom was killed and David's heart was broken. He wept and mourned for Absalom whom he loved but allowed to be estranged. "O my son, Absalom! My son, my son Absalom!" David had failed as a father, and the fruit of his own sins were crushing his heart. How could he go on?

David's failure as a father is different in many ways from the *burnout* situations that we face in the ministry today. But the fact that he continued to passionately seek intimacy with God in the midst of it all is an exhortation to us. Surely, only someone who had burned out as a father and in his ministry as the leader of God's people, as David had, could say with integrity and authority that God was able to restore his soul.

> *The LORD is my shepherd, I shall not be in want. He makes me lie down in green pastures, he leads me beside quiet waters, he restores my soul. He guides me in paths of righteousness for his name's sake. (Psalms 23:1-3)*

## REPENTANCE, MERCY AND A PLACE OF REFUGE

It is obvious that David's sins, his rebellious heart and his own terrible choices were the reasons for the pressure, pain and affliction that he bore. Perhaps, in his eyes, managing a kingdom was easier than the primary responsibilities of loving one wife and caring for his children as a godly father. He also failed as a king, and it is clear that the overwhelming circumstances that he faces are of his own design. For that reason God's mercy toward him is striking and glorious in our eyes, and it brings such comfort and hope to our hearts. Many of us struggle with pressures and pains that are the result of our choices and failures.

Just as God pursued Elijah in his battles, He sought David in his sin. It was God's eternal love for David that moved Him to send Nathan to seek David's repentance. When the prophet confronted David with his sin, he responded thus:

> *Then David said to Nathan, "I have sinned against the LORD." Nathan replied, "The LORD has taken away your sin. You are not going to die." (2 Samuel 12:13)*

David expanded on his repentance in his great prayer of bro-kenness in Psalm 51.

*Have mercy on me, O God, according to your unfailing love; according to your great compassion blot out my transgressions. Wash away all my iniquity and cleanse me from my sin. (Psalms 51:1,2)*

David cried out to God for mercy and for his heavenly Father to wash his sins away. He did not hide his transgressions from God, but openly confessed his sin and God's righteous judgments.

*For I know my transgressions, and my sin is always before me. Against you, you only, have I sinned and done what is evil in your sight, so that you are proved right when you speak and justified when you judge. (Psalms 51:3,4)*

In God's mercy, He became a refuge for David. Our only hope in the midst of our pressures, failures and sins is to flee to the same God who became a sanctuary for David's heart.

*In you, O LORD, I have taken refuge; let me never be put to shame; deliver me in your righteousness. Turn your ear to me, come quickly to my rescue; be my rock of refuge, a strong fortress to save me. (Psalms 31:1,2)*

David's teaching is very visual. God is a refuge, a rock and a fortress, but above all, it is His glorious presence that becomes our hiding place when the pressure and pain are more than we can bear. This was David's testimony.

*In the shelter of your presence you hide them from the intrigues of men; in your dwelling you keep them safe from the strife of tongues. (Psalms 31:20)*

Many of David's most powerful and beautiful songs of worship were born in the midst of his pain and affliction. It was as he was fleeing from Saul and from Absalom that David ran to the God who had become his shepherd in those long days and nights when he watched the sheep. The Person of God became the place in which

David lived when the terrors of the battles confronted him and when he was alone, afraid and confused. It was God who became his shelter and his fortress, his rock and his refuge.

> *Since you are my rock and my fortress, for the sake of your name lead and guide me. Free me from the trap that is set for me, for you are my refuge. Into your hands I commit my spirit; redeem me, O LORD, the God of truth. (Psalms 31:3-5)*

David knew that God had set His affections upon him, and for the sake of God's own reputation and His great Name, his Father would give him the direction, the freedom, the deliverance and the redemption he needed.

## THE SONGS OF A LOVER

It is no wonder that David loved God the way he did. God's mercy in the midst of his sin, God's protection when he was surrounded by enemies, and God's strength in the midst of his weakness became the framework of his life. It was in the crucible of David's trials and in the pain he bore that his psalms of worship were born. The way in which God poured Himself out to David stimulated in his heart a passionate response to His Father. In fact, the only way we can describe David's relationship with God is that it was a lover's relationship.

> *I will extol the LORD at all times; his praise will always be on my lips. My soul will boast in the LORD; let the afflicted hear and rejoice. Glorify the LORD with me; let us exalt his name together. (Psalms 34:1-3)*

The praises of his beloved were always on David's lips and His name the delight of his heart. Later in this psalm, David exhorts the reader to "taste and see that the Lord is good" (v. 8). The song in Psalm 27 reveals the intimate expressions of a lover!

*One thing I ask of the LORD, this is what I seek: that I may dwell in the house of the LORD all the days of my life, to gaze upon the beauty of the LORD and to seek him in his temple. (Psalms 27:4)*

David's desires were inflamed; his passions were heightened. In all of his being, David was stimulated and his hungers were awakened to find fulfillment in God alone. He continues in this way:

*Hear my voice when I call, O LORD; be merciful to me and answer me. My heart says of you, "Seek his face!" Your face, LORD, I will seek. (Psalms 27:7,8)*

Although Psalm 42 does not bear David's name, Charles Spurgeon has an explanation:

*Although David is not mentioned as the author, this Psalm must be the offspring of his pen; it is so Davidic, it smells of the son of Jesse, it bears the marks of his style and experience in every letter. We could sooner doubt the authorship of the second part of Pilgrim's Progress than question David's title to be the composer of this Psalm.[1]*

We witness in these words again the heart of a lover.

*As the deer pants for streams of water, so my soul pants for you, O God. My soul thirsts for God, for the living God. When can I go and meet with God? (Psalms 42:1,2)*

David's life with God was a passionate love relationship. When we read his songs, we are reminded once again that this is the kind of relationship that God desires with us. He is our Lover and we are His beloved. God hungers for a deep and intimate, passion-

---

1  C.H. Spurgeon, *The Treasury of David*, Funk & Wagnalls, New York, 1882, p. 299.

filled lover's relationship, flowing out of the truth of Himself which He reveals to us, and the way He gives Himself to us.

## OUR PASSIONS AND OUR MINISTRIES

Our lives and our ministries do not flow primarily out of our insights. All that we are and all that we do flow first out of our passions and desires. God has designed us to be passionate people and to find our fulfillment in Him alone.

In his great treatise on *The Religious Affections*, Jonathan Edwards says the following:

> *If we be not in good earnest in religion, and our wills and inclinations be not strongly exercised, we are nothing. The things of religion are so great, that there can be no suit - ableness in the exercises of our hearts to their nature and importance, unless they be lively and powerful.* [2]

Edwards tells us that the exercises of our hearts must be powerfully engaged if we would be "earnest in religion." He contin - ues thus:

> *And such, when they receive the Spirit of God in his sanctifying and saving influences, are said to be "baptized with the Holy Ghost, and with fire," by reason of the power and fervour of those exercises the Spirit of God excites in their hearts, whereby their hearts, when grace is in exer- cise, may be said to "burn within them;" as is said of the disciples, Luke xxiv.32.* [3]

---

2 Jonathan Edwards, *The Religious Affections*, The Banner of Truth Trust, Carlisle, PA, 1746, p. 28.
3 *The Religious Affections*, p. 28.

He tells us that it was the exercises of the Holy Spirit that excited the hearts of the disciples within them. It was His grace which caused their hearts to burn. Edwards goes on as follows:

> ...*wherever true religion is, there are vigorous exercises of the inclination and will towards divine objects: but by what was said before, the vigorous, lively, and sensible exercises of the will, are no other than the affections of the soul.*[4]

True religion flows out of the affections of the soul! In the Church today we do not speak much about affections, about hearts burning with excitement for God, or about intimacy. We speak much more about principles and insights. We talk a great deal about priorities, goals and objectives. Planning in the ministry is not only proper, it is essential; but we tend to place our hope in these rather than ministry flowing from the intimacy of our rela - tionship with God. I want to share with you why I think this is so and one of the main reasons many of us are drying up in the ministry.

## WE ARE INSIGHT-DRIVEN

When God placed Adam and Eve in the Garden of Eden, He gave them an environment of beauty and fullness in which to enjoy the wonders of His creation and even to be His co-workers, as they would stimulate what He had made to fruitfulness. There were two trees in the middle of the garden, the Tree of Life and the Tree of the Knowledge of Good and Evil. God called Adam and Eve to eat from the Tree of Life. God Himself would be the source of all that

---

4 *The Religious Affections*, p. 29.

they needed on every level of their lives. Spiritually, intellectually, emotionally and physically, God would pour Himself into them as they partook of that tree. But God forbade them to eat from the Tree of the Knowledge of Good and Evil. In fact, He warned them that if they did, they would die.

As God called Adam and Eve to eat from the Tree of Life and forbade them to eat of the Tree of the Knowledge of Good and Evil, we find one of the most basic, protective truths of all time. God was telling them, "It is better to know me than to possess the sum of all the knowledge and information that this world can give to you." But Adam and Eve ate from the wrong tree, and every generation since has made the same choice. We are still feeding on the Tree of the Knowledge of Good and Evil.

What is the fruit of our choices? Today we are living in the midst of the greatest explosion of knowledge that this world has ever seen. In fact, we cannot assimilate knowledge as fast as we are gaining it. In the fields of computers, medicine, and space exploration, we have become overwhelmed by the infor - mation that we possess.

However, has all of that knowledge and information made any difference in the human heart? Has it affected what is happening in the war-torn and poverty-stricken areas of this world? Has it brought justice and peace to enslaved peoples? Not at all! With all of our knowledge, the heart of man is still becoming more and more depraved with every passing gen - eration.

It was in the Garden of Eden that we sacrificed intimacy for information. Since that day we have become insight-driven. God has called us to find fulfillment in relationships of life—with Him and with one another. However, because of the fall, we fear intimacy and pursue information.

## THE BIRTH OF FORMULA RELIGION

The fall in the Garden of Eden also brought to us the birth of pragmatism and formula religion. Ever since Satan said to Eve, "You do this and you will be like God," we have been convinced that if someone tells us how to do something, we can accomplish it. We are convinced that we have within ourselves all of the resources we need; it is the "how to" we are missing. That is why formulas for the Christian life and simplistic procedures for building ministries are so appealing to us. "Ten steps to a successful marriage" or "Twelve principles for growing a church" are far more attractive to us than the call to seek God and to trust Him even in the dark times.

I was sharing these thoughts recently with a brother in the pastoral ministry. "It is interesting to me as a pastor that the two things people want most from me are insight into something that God is doing and a formula to get out of the pain and struggle of maturity. The mysterious workings of God often do not allow me to give either one."

The trouble with pragmatism—the mindset that if it works it is right—is that it does appear to be successful. While it makes a great deal of sense and in some ways it gets the job done, we may lose more in the process than we gain. While great things are happening around us, even though they might not last for long, we might very well be drying up inside and burning out. The inner core of our person is sustained only by intimacy with God, and out of that intimacy flows His life and His works which will transform our people on an eternal level.

I remember well a seminary professor who had a powerful influence on me. I was gripped by the depth of his heart for God. He told us, "Always minister out of the overflow of your own relationship with God." God used that call to stir my own heart toward God.

What is your relationship with God like? Is He a visitor in your life, a counselor or a teacher? Or is He your lover?! Is your relationship characterized by knowledge alone, or is it filled with hunger, passion and intimacy? What is your first waking thought in the morning? Who do you think of most frequently in your free time? How much time do you spend with God in His Word and in daily prayer? Do your sermon applications deal with the heart issues of your people?

David, even with all of his failure and sin, became a man after God's own heart. His responsive heart before the Lord and his passionate hunger for intimacy with God enabled him to endure even the most devastating afflictions, pressure and pain. When we learn to serve our people out of the overflow of our intimacy with God, our hearts will remain full, and they will be transformed in His presence. May God make us lovers of Him above all else and keep us by His grace from sacrificing intimacy for insight, as appealing as that may be in our present circumstances.

## REFLECTIONS, COMMITMENTS AND PRAYER

*God, would You stir within me a passion for Yourself like You gave to David? Would You "enflame the affections of my soul" and focus them all on the beauty of Your face? Please keep me from being driven by the formulas and principles of this pragmatic system at the expense of intimacy with You. Make me Your lover above all else, Lord, and out of that intimacy cause Your life to flow which will sustain me and transform those around me.*

# SECTION 2

# The Road to Burnout: Losing Our Bearings

*The Lord delights in the way of the man whose steps he has made firm; though he stumble, he will not fall, for the LORD upholds him with his hand.*

*Psalms 37:23,24*

*How long, O LORD, must I call for help, but you do not listen?*
*Or cry out to you, "Violence!" but you do not save?*

*Habakkuk 1:2*

# 4

## *Habakkuk: When God Disappoints Us*

**G**od *does* disappoint us at times. Rather consistently, He fails to meet our expectations of what we think He ought to do. God has a way of surprising us, bringing circumstances and crises into our lives that are unexpected and which have unpredictable conse- quences. In this chapter, we will observe the way in which Habak- kuk responded to his deep disappointments with God. How did he not burn out when confronted with the silences of God? How did he keep going when God seemed to be acting in unjust ways? We will discover the way in which Habakkuk moved from self-confi - dence to brokenness before the Lord and how, simultaneously, his understanding of God expanded dramatically. In the end, we will see a man of God who was able to trust and even rejoice in Him, in spite of the terrible circumstances swirling around him.

## Our Cultural Decline

*Burnout* is primarily an "inner disease," yet it is often stimulated or exacerbated by outside influences. Ministry disappointment can easily turn into *burnout* as co-workers and others fail us, or as growth doesn't happen as quickly as we expect. In addition, the larger culture in which we live can also wear on us, draining us of energy and hope: a perfect precursor to *burnout*. Here was Habakkuk's struggle: a godly man living within a culture bent on sin and moving ever so swiftly away from the things of God. As Habakkuk surveyed the scene, he began to lose heart. In desperation, he cried out to the Lord:

> *How long, O LORD, must I call for help, but you do not listen? Or cry out to you, "Violence!" but you do not save? (Habakkuk 1:2)*

Since Habakkuk had been watching this cultural and social decline for some time, this was not a new problem, nor was this the first time he had spoken to the Lord about his concerns. He had been watching his people, Judah, move further and further away from the way of holiness. As a faithful prophet, he had repeatedly asked God to check this slide toward depravity but with no apparent success, for the decline continued unabated. With a note of frustration and weariness, Habakkuk complained to God: "How long, O Lord?"

As far as Habakkuk was concerned, the Lord was not acting quickly enough. After all, he had been praying for weeks or months or even years. How long did God expect him keep on praying? He wanted to know, "Why isn't God working *now*?"

Although we have sensed this frustration with the trends in our own culture, if we are honest, we must admit that our frustration is as much with God as it is with our politicians and media/entertainment mavens. God *could* be doing something about our national decline. If He is the great Sovereign over the nations, which He is, then why hasn't He responded sooner?

The fact is, He has not. Rather, our society seems to be spiraling downward more quickly than ever. We appear to be losing the Culture Wars. One moral barrier after another is collapsing before the onslaught of a radical concept of tolerance. Previously sacro - sanct notions of sexuality are being discarded at a breathtaking rate. Our culture, having rejected any transcendent basis for mo - rality, has discovered that the seemingly impregnable walls protect- ing marriage, family and civil relationships are porous, or simply an illusion, like the scenery on a set which depicts a fortress with insurmountable defenses, but which in fact is made of nothing more than flimsy, painted muslin cloth.

Doesn't it worry you as you consider the world which your children and grandchildren will inherit? We plead, "How long, O Lord, how long?" This was Habakkuk's cry as well. "Why, Lord, aren't you listening to me? I know You can do it. I know You want to do it. So, why aren't You doing it?" Habakkuk is in danger of *burnout*, uncertain that he can continue to wait, uncertain that he can continue to pray, as God remains silent.

## WHY ARE YOU TOLERATING THIS?

*Why do you make me look at injustice? Why do you tolerate wrong? Destruction and violence are before me; there is strife, and conflict abounds. (Habakkuk 1:3)*

The second great question Habakkuk asks is "why?" "Why, Lord, do you tolerate wrong?" Habakkuk is like a social scientist, observing the trends of his day. Unfortunately, the parallels to our present day are all too obvious.

Habakkuk observed a Judah that was in the midst of social upheaval. The government agencies which were supposed to insure security for the populace were failing. Violence was on the rise. Anti-social behavior was becoming more the rule than the excep - tion. Habakkuk seems to be describing our own country!

However, Habakkuk despaired not only over raw violence but also over a more diffuse and widespread demeanor which was infecting his society. Civility and generosity were being replaced by strife and conflict. Trust was being supplanted by suspicion. Social scientists in our day have documented similar trends in the U.S. [1] People don't trust one another, and they certainly don't trust organizations and institutions.

This broader cultural trend has infected our churches as well. To learn of churches or pastors being sued no longer shocks us. Even within the church, we are losing our capacity to handle disagreements in love and to treat one another with respect, civility and trust. As pastors, this malaise of mistrust further erodes our spirits, making us more vulnerable to *burnout* than ever.

Habakkuk describes other disturbing trends which are deeply troubling to the prophet and a great offense to God. The prophet decries injustice, greed, robbery, and extortion (Hab. 1:4; 2: 6,7,9) and laments the debauchery of the day.

> *Woe to him who gives drink to his neighbors, pouring it from the wineskin till they are drunk, so that he can gaze on their naked bodies. (Habakkuk 2:15)*

## THE SILENCES OF GOD

Our situation in the United States at the end of the 20th century bears a remarkable resemblance to Judah in 610 B.C. Violence is a national scourge; mistrust and cynicism are pandemic; justice is

---

1 *The Washington Post*, 1/28/96, Section A.

increasingly attained only for a price. Immorality and other personal excesses are becoming normative. How is one pastor able to stand against such overwhelming cultural decay? How is one church supposed to make a difference? Unfortunately, our churches are not immune to the cultural trends we see. The huge problems which our nation is facing are not simply "out there." The problems, the evils we have described, often touch close to home. Our own people too easily succumb to these same pressures and temptations and are swept up in the sins of the larger culture.

How was Habakkuk to "keep on keeping on" while sin was on the rise and righteousness was in retreat? What he desperately needed was God's perspective and God's assurance that righteous - ness would prevail. But all Habakkuk heard was silence. Where was God in the midst of this mounting evil? Where was the Lord of Hosts, the high and lofty One of Israel? Why was He not doing anything? Why was He taking so long? Why did He not speak?

When have you struggled with the silences of God? When has God disappointed you with His failure to act? When have you prayed for individuals, perhaps even members of your own family, only to see them destroyed by sin? We are most vulnerable to *burnout* at this very point. When we seek God's face for those things which are undoubtedly *good*, such as healing or deliverance for a friend, a marriage or a family, and then see nothing but failure, we begin to despair. How do we account for God's inaction? Why has He not come in power with "a mighty hand and outstretched arm?" (Ps. 136:12)

One of the greatest disappointments of my life has been the divorce of a couple very dear to my wife and me. We so loved this couple and greatly enjoyed spending a week or two with them each year. We began to hear about difficulties in their marriage and began to pray regularly for them. I remember one morning finding a passage in Isaiah which spoke of God preserving "a bruised reed" and a "smoldering wick" (Isa. 42:3). I claimed this verse as a promise for them and their marriage; I was so encouraged that God had given to me a personal word to pray over and to claim on their behalf. And pray I did. I probably prayed more fervently and more faithfully for them than I have for anything else in my life. I had full confidence that God was going to restore their relationship.

He didn't. The marriage dissolved and the questions arose. "Why, God, did You remain silent? You could have easily brought healing to them. You surely could have preserved the smoldering wick of their relationship. I know that this was Your will. Why, God, did you fail to act?"

Over ten years later I still don't have answers to these questions. If we are honest, we must admit that God's failure to act in specific situations is one of the great perplexities of our lives. His "failures" can become a precursor to our *burnout*. How are we to respond to our disappointments with God? The book of Habakkuk points the way, but the path still has unexpected twists and turns ahead.

### INCONCEIVABLE!

For how long did Habakkuk endure the divine silence? Months? Years? At long last, Habakkuk received an answer from the Lord, but it was an answer that left him more confused and discouraged than ever.

> *Look at the nations and watch—and be utterly amazed. For I am going to do something in your days that you would not believe, even if you were told. (Habakkuk 1:5)*

God says, in effect, "Get ready, Habakkuk, for I have been preparing a fitting response that is going to amaze you. It's big, Habakkuk, much bigger than what you had in mind. It's not just about Judah; it's international; it's global!"

*I am raising up the Babylonians, that ruthless and impetuous people, who sweep across the whole earth to seize dwelling places not their own. (Habakkuk 1:6)*

The Babylonians! A pagan nation from the east, a rising world power, the nation that had broken the Assyrian stranglehold on that part of the world that had lasted seven centuries. Babylon, a nation of warriors that are "feared and dreaded" whose "horses are swifter than leopards, fiercer than wolves at dusk." The Babyloni - ans who "fly like a vulture swooping to devour" and "come bent on violence." The Babylonian army whose "calvary gallops headlong" and whose "hordes advance like a desert wind" (Hab. 1:7-9).

God could not have described a more terrifying scene to Habakkuk. The images of leopards, wolves, vultures, hordes ad - vancing are powerful and evocative. Habakkuk must have been shell-shocked listening to the grisly description of the nation which would come to Judah and "laugh at all fortified cities...build earthen ramps and capture them." The picture of Babylon blasting into Judah and "gathering prisoners like sand" must have caused Habakkuk's heart to sink (Hab. 1:9-10).

God made it perfectly clear that this judgment was directly from His hand. "I am raising up the Babylonians." Judah was not simply a pawn upon the chessboard of Middle Eastern history who hap - pened to get caught up in a geopolitical struggle. No! God was doing this. He was marshaling the Babylonians to destroy Judah!

## MORE THAN WE BARGAIN FOR

Habakkuk got far more than he bargained for. Although he had asked God to judge the sins of Judah, after hearing of the intensity and completeness of the judgment, he was left stunned! C.S. Lewis' words would be so apt for Habakkuk:

*The great spirit you so lightly invoked, the "lord of the terrible aspect," is present: not a senile benevolence that drowsily wishes you to be happy in your own way, not the cold philanthropy of a conscientious magistrate, not the care of a host who feels responsible for the comfort of his guests, but the consuming fire Himself...* [2]

We can almost see Habakkuk's mind spinning as he tries to articulate his confusion.

*O LORD, are you not from everlasting? My God, my Holy One, we will not die. O LORD, you have appointed them to execute judgment; O Rock, you have ordained them to punish. (Habakkuk 1:12)*

Habakkuk has been struck by both the fierceness of the coming judgment and by the means which God was going to use, namely a pagan, proud, godless nation. This isn't the God who Habakkuk thought he knew. He tried reminding God that He is from everlasting, Yahweh, the covenant-keeping God. How could He destroy His own people so thoroughly? How could God use "guilty men, whose own strength is their god?" (Hab. 1:11). The Lord's response was creating a huge disconnect with Habakkuk's theology.

## TELLING GOD WHAT HE SHOULD DO

*Your eyes are too pure to look on evil; you cannot tolerate wrong. Why then do you tolerate the treacherous? Why are you silent while the wicked swallow up those more righteous than themselves? (Habakkuk 1:13)*

---

2  C.S. Lewis, *The Problem of Pain*, Geoffrey, Bles, London, 1956, p. 35.

From Habakkuk's perspective, God was about to act in a way completely inconsistent with His character. Habakkuk had earlier complained that God was "tolerating wrong" in Judah (Hab. 1:3), but now God is going even further by "tolerating the treacherous." To Habakkuk this hardly seems to be a fitting response by the Holy One, the Rock.

We all hold expectations regarding what God should and should not do. We carry certain expectations of the way in which He should grow the church, not only numerically but also in terms of maturity, vision, and love. We have expectations of the way our children should turn out. These are *good* expectations, fully consistent with what we see revealed in the Scriptures. Yet, often, God doesn't do that which He "obviously" *ought* to do. If we are honest, we must admit that often we are disappointed in what God does or in what He fails to do. We pray for worship services in which the presence of God is so apparent and real that our people are energized to worship with wholehearted devotion. Surely, this is God's will, but instead, worship once again falls short. We pray for a man to be delivered from drugs or alcohol, (what could be more in God's will than this?) yet in the end these things destroy him. The fact is, God often doesn't perform as we think He ought.

## THE PERFECT SOLUTION

The ministry of Leadership Resources faced a severe disappointment with God's ways a few years ago. In the aftermath of that disappointment, we have been challenged to live out our theol ogy—will we trust God in the midst of our deep disappointments?

Since its inception, the ministry of Leadership Resources has operated out of the home of its president and founder, Bill Mills. Over the last decade, the ministry has been expanding and outgrow ing the Mills' basement and home. We began seeking a separate headquarters building, and a few years ago thought we had found the perfect solution. Just a few miles from the Mills' home was an old farmhouse with a double barn which could easily have been converted into an office and production area, just the perfect size for our needs. It was located on a beautiful piece of property overlooking a forest preserve. We reached agreement with the owner and signed a contract, contingent on obtaining the requisite zoning approvals. Our rehab designs envisioned a building rich in ambiance and warmth without being pretentious; it seemed to really fit the ministry both in terms of physical space and also in terms of "feel."

Zoning required five different approvals. With the help of influential friends we easily breezed through the first three meetings. It was obvious to all that God was giving us this wonderful gift. In the fourth meeting, the door slammed shut—our zoning request was denied. We were stunned.

This bitter disappointment became a crisis for the ministry. We could have easily burned out and lost heart. We could not understand "why." Why did God seem to clearly lead us (our staff and board of directors were without exception very enthusiastic about this move) and then change direction at the last minute?

It has been a humbling experience for me personally. I have grown less confident of my ability to predict what God is going to do. I had been *certain*, beyond any shadow of doubt, that the Lord was giving us this barn, but I was wrong. God was doing something else. He is not beholden to my plans; He has His own agenda, to which I am beholden. My desire is that my confidence not be rooted in what I think God ought to do, but rather in God Himself, apart from how He performs on my behalf.

God is about to answer Habakkuk's complaint about proud Babylon, but before He does, He reminds Habakkuk of how He expects His children to respond in the midst of their disappointments with God.

*See, he is puffed up; his desires are not upright—but the righteous will live by his faith. (Habakkuk 2:4)*

Sometimes God provides answers and sometimes He does not. In either event, He calls us to trust Him and to trust that He has a larger view of life than we do. We are called to trust Him, even in spite of our confusion and disappointments. We are called to pursue His purposes, even when our own dreams fail to material - ize.

Habakkuk is going to come around to God's agenda in the end and even be able to rejoice in it. In the meantime, however, he continues to struggle with the "lord of the terrible aspect," trusting Him while waiting for an adequate answer.

## WAITING FOR AN ANSWER

*I will stand at my watch and station myself on the ramparts; I will look to see what he will say to me, and what answer I am to give to this complaint. (Habakkuk 2:1)*

God responded a second time to Habakkuk. After Judah's judgment is complete, Babylon will herself be judged.

*Because you have plundered many nations, the peoples who are left will plunder you. For you have shed man's blood; you have destroyed lands and cities and everyone in them. (Habakkuk 2:8)*

Though God is going to use Babylon's ruthlessness and cruelty to bring a just judgment on Judah, this in no way excuses her excesses. Babylon will pay dearly for her manifold sins. Babylon is full of "guilty men whose own strength is their god" (Hab. 1:11). They will soon discover that their gods are inadequate to deliver them from the wrath of the true and living God. Because they have "promoted their own honor" (Hab. 1:7) and have been "puffed up" (Hab. 2:4), God will bring them low.

God describes five different woes which He will wield in judgment. Within the text there is some ambiguity as to whom these woes refer. Several of the judgments point directly to Babylon and her leaders, yet others seem directed toward Judah or even toward Assyria which had recently been conquered and supplanted by Babylon. Some of the warnings focus on individuals while others address groups and nations.

## WHO ARE THE "BAD GUYS?"

Who is the *real* enemy? Though Habakkuk began by seeing the unrighteous of Judah as the enemy, after God announced the judgment via Babylon, Habakkuk shifted allegiances and began siding with Judah as those "more righteous than" Babylon (Hab. 1:13). Habakkuk saw his unrighteous countrymen as bad, but not really *that* bad, and certainly not as bad as pagan Babylon. His ethnocentricities seemed to have "kicked in" as God's impending judgment advanced.

The Church in the U.S. struggles with this same ambivalence. How do we view the pagans among us? On one hand, we are angry and disappointed with the spreading moral decay in our country. On the other hand, we love our country and feel proud of it. When we sense the country is threatened or challenged, we rise up to defend her. How would we respond if God were to raise up a wicked nation to humble or defeat our country? We surely would be able to identify with Habakkuk. Like him, we would struggle with our understanding of God and His righteous workings in the world.

Who is the *real* enemy? What is God's perspective on this question? The fact is His enemies are not defined by national

94

boundaries nor by ethnic or racial affiliation nor by political philosophy nor even (in one sense) by religious identity. All those who follow the Son are His friends; all others are His enemies. In this sense, *all* of the nations are His enemies.

> *Has not the LORD Almighty determined that the people's labor is only fuel for the fire, that the nations exhaust themselves for nothing? (Habakkuk 2:13)*

His Kingdom operates on a totally different paradigm than the kingdoms of the world. God is bringing in His kingdom, a kingdom of redeemed people. To those outside the kingdom, He gives much common grace, but in the final analysis, they are His enemies and deserving of judgment. God's great commitment (His covenant) is to His chosen people, to those who seek His glory.

## THE TRAGEDY OF LESSER CAUSES

> *For the earth will be filled with the knowledge of the glory of the LORD, as the waters cover the sea. (Habakkuk 2:14)*

Here is God's great priority. He calls His people to this agenda and to no other: the glory of God filling the earth. Herein is a key to battling *burnout*. His agenda alone is worthy of our calling and certain of fulfillment. Any other agenda is a lesser one and ultimately a distraction from the Great Cause. As Solomon discovered, the plans and activities of men have no enduring value. Only what God does endures forever (Ecc. 3:14). God undertakes His activities on earth "so that men will revere him" (Ecc. 3:15). Displaying His own glory is His ultimate goal. *Burnout* is inevitable if we attach our aspirations and identities to lesser causes which bear no eternal fruit and to which our God is not committed.

Portions of the evangelical church have adopted a political agenda. As we tie our hopes to this agenda, we are bound to be disappointed. During the Clinton presidency, we have seen a mal -

95

aise spread over the evangelical church, at times bordering on despair. Have we too closely identified with a party, with an agenda, with a kingdom of this world? The congresses, the political parties, the parliaments, the governments of the world all stand under the judgment of God. Though senators speechify and presidents prom - ise and politicians boast, only the kingdom of our Lord and His Christ will remain.

Chapter two of Habakkuk is filled with the activities of men and nations. It describes powerful military campaigns destroying lands and cities, economic systems creating great wealth for individuals, religious systems attempting to provide answers to life's questions. In the midst of this furious hubbub, this clattering of activity, a clear voice cries out, "Silence!"

> *But the LORD is in his holy temple; let all the earth be silent before him." (Habakkuk 2:20)*

Suddenly the perspective changes from the noisy, restless activity of men on earth to the very presence of God in heaven. As Habakkuk prays his third and final prayer, its tone is starkly different from the others, spoken with a hushed voice. Habakkuk has a sense of standing in that glorious temple before the presence of the awesome King.

> *LORD, I have heard of your fame; I stand in awe of your deeds, O LORD. Renew them in our day, in our time make them known; in wrath remember mercy. (Habakkuk 3:2)*

Standing before this great King, Habakkuk demands nothing. He makes no accusations regarding God's justice. He does not question whether God is doing right or not. He doesn't try to change or delay God's intended purposes but rather encourages God to act soon. Whereas earlier, Habakkuk wanted *less* of God's activity, now he wants *more*. Habakkuk invites God (not that God needed an invitation!) to play out all of His purposes, even if there is to be great pain in the process. Habakkuk's only caveat is neither a demand nor a negotiating stance, but rather a plea: "remember mercy."

Earlier, Habakkuk had had a clear sense of what God ought or ought not do. He wanted God to judge Judah, but with a modest judgment. He then went on to challenge God when the Lord promised to unleash an overwhelming chastisement. Habakkuk felt free to tell God how He ought to do His business, acting as if it were his birthright to tell God what to do and how to do it. Perhaps Habakkuk had "control" issues in his life!

We, too, as pastors and leaders often think that we know how things ought to be done. After all, we're professionals! Perhaps we grow frustrated when board members oppose our ideas. Just as Habakkuk saw certain people in Judah as obstacles to the things of God, perhaps we too grouse about some of our people, our "thorns in the flesh." In almost every church there are one or two individuals that "minister" to the pastor by questioning or challenging his every move. Most churches also have one or two families which consume extraordinary amounts of time and energy. We are tempted to tell God how to fix these "problems." Similar to Habak-kuk, we may even ask God to judge an individual or group within the church.

## A MATTER OF PERSPECTIVE

These *problems* may look very different from the perspective of the heavenlies. What if these people are part of God's process in our lives and in the lives of our churches? Perhaps they are even part of God's "severe mercies" in our lives. Are we able to welcome *all* of the mighty acts of God, even the bitter ones? Don't we want *more* of God, regardless of what that *more* might bring?

In chapter one Habakkuk was operating from an earthbound perspective. The Lord responded by presenting a larger and fuller understanding of history, of good and evil, of His purposes, and of Himself. The Lord presented a series of elevations, each one higher than the previous one. Habakkuk was at first standing at ground level, viewing life from a limited perspective. In His first response, the Lord presented a higher view of the region encompassing Judah and Babylon. In the second response, the Lord spoke from an even higher elevation, addressing all of the nations with the intention that His glory fill all the earth. Finally, the Lord presented a vision of Himself in His holy temple far above a silent and awestruck earth. This is the vantage point which Habakkuk was lacking and which he needed so much, a perspective that in the end changed his life and ministry.

Habakkuk's prayer in chapter three reflects a remarkable transformation. He is now viewing life and ministry from that higher elevation, from the perspective of heaven itself.

*God came from Teman, the Holy One from Mount Paran. His glory covered the heavens and his praise filled the earth. His splendor was like the sunrise; rays flashed from his hand, where his power was hidden. (Habakkuk 3:3,4)*

We find safety from *burnout* at this higher elevation. Our understanding and our perspective are sharpened as we view life and ministry from the vantage point of heaven. From ground level life appears chaotic, and our perspective is like that of a foot soldier engaged in a deadly skirmish: problems may seem insurmountable, crises may seem out of control, enemies may seem all-pow - erful, the cause may appear to be lost. However, the perspective quickly changes as we move up the hill overlooking the battlefield upon which the commander can clearly see that the battle is, indeed, being won.

From the perspective of the heavenlies we do see the battle being won. We can see our Sovereign Lord intimately involved in the affairs of life and fulfilling His great, overarching purpose of filling the earth with His glory. We see a "God on the move." In chapter one, Habakkuk complained that God wasn't doing anything. In chapter three, he recognizes that God has been at work all the time as the Author of history, which can only be explained by God's direct intervention in the affairs of men and nations.

From below, the finger of God remains invisible to our eyes, and often we are unable to see the patterns of life. Nevertheless, God is weaving the affairs of our lives and the lives of those around us into His tapestry. Our pain, failures, disappointments, and even our sin are all part of this great and glorious work. God, in His manifold wisdom, even weaves our flaws into His tapestry with such great skill that the result remains flawless, precisely according to His all-wise and all-knowing design. We are able to find great freedom as we entrust to God that His perspective on life and ministry is the correct one.

## THE SEVERE MERCIES OF GOD

In the beginning Habakkuk was focused on Judah; next his focus became Babylon; but now Habakkuk is looking at the Lord, harkening back to the God of Sinai. This isn't a God with whom one negotiates, nor is He merely Judah's private God. He is a God who comes with power, who shakes the earth, who makes the nations tremble, whose ways are eternal. By way of graphic illus - tration, Habakkuk pictures a howling, devastating storm which sweeps across the land. The sea rages, the mountains writhe, the sun and moon stand still (Hab. 3:6-11). Within this picture, he sees the unrestrained wrath of God, yet a wrath which contains the seeds of salvation.

Habakkuk is reminding his people of God's glorious deliverances of Israel in the past, particularly the Exodus experience and the defeat of the Canaanites at the Kishon River (Judges 4-5.) What a timely and powerful reminder! Acts of deliverance such as these were God's monuments to be treasured as a reminder of His continual provision and unfailing love.

When have you seen a great deliverance of God? What were those personal deliverances in your life and the individual and family deliverances within your church? What are your "Ebenezers," the experiences of life upon which you declare, "thus far has the Lord helped us" (1 Sam. 7:12)? Our own histories are replete with the merciful acts of God. These memories are a strong foundation upon which to stand when the wrath of God is swirling about us, and we find it difficult to get perspective and to understand the larger story. At last Habakkuk identifies the greater purpose of God's wrath—He is intent upon saving His elect.

> *In wrath you strode through the earth and in anger you threshed the nations. You came out to deliver your people, to save your anointed one. (Habakkuk 3:12,13a)*

God will not tolerate the present condition of His people. He shares Habakkuk's despair over their waywardness, and He loves Judah too much to allow them to remain in their woeful state. His cleansing, healing wrath is about to come. "God's love is not a mindless sentimentality. It is a purifying fire, a force in the strongest opposition to everything that mars those whom God loves....God's wrath is God's love blazing out in fiery indignation against every evil in the beloved."[3]

---

3 Leon Morris, *The Atonement: Its Meaning and Significance*, IVP, Downers Grove, IL, 1983, pp. 163,174.

## WHEN CALAMITY COMES

*I heard and my heart pounded, my lips quivered at the sound;
decay crept into my bones, and my legs trembled. Yet I will wait
patiently for the day of calamity to come on the nation invading
us. (Habakkuk 3:16)*

Habakkuk is shaken to his very core. God's words have come
to him with great power and deep conviction so that Habakkuk is
trembling, terrified, afraid of what is about to happen; his mind is
awhirl, though in one way he understands what God is saying, but
on the other hand, he doesn't.

Habakkuk will wait. God has said that after Judah is consumed
by Babylon, Babylon herself will be condemned. When will this be?
Certainly not immediately, perhaps not even in Habakkuk's own
lifetime. Nevertheless, he will wait patiently for God to fulfill His
word. Here Habakkuk clearly aligns himself with God and His
agenda. Habakkuk has no further protests or complaints but has
accepted as good what God is about to do. Habakkuk has caught
a glimpse of God's glory, of His faithfulness in the past, of His
goodness in the present, and of His glorious purposes in the future.
Habakkuk has seen God and that is enough. He will wait patiently
for all that is about to unfold.

William Carey, "the father of modern missions," also faced a
ministry disappointment of overwhelming proportions. Only by
resting in God's sovereign purposes was he, like Habakkuk, able
to endure and not burn out. Carey began his missionary career to
India in 1793. He labored in that country for forty continuous years,
never once returning to his native England. Carey was a brilliant
linguist, translating portions of Scripture into over a dozen Indian
languages. One afternoon after twenty years of plodding labor in
that country, all of his work went up in smoke. A fire raged through
his printing plant and warehouse. All of his printing equipment was

destroyed, but most tragically, many of his precious manuscripts were completely consumed by the fire. Of course, Carey had no computer back-up files or Xerox masters. Twenty years of non-stop labor were gone within a few hours.

How would he respond to this crushing devastation? How would you respond in similar circumstances? Listen to the words which Carey wrote to his pastor-friend, Andrew Fuller, in England:

> *The ground must be laboured over again, but we are not discouraged...We have all been supported under the affliction, and preserved from discouragement. To me the con - sideration of the divine sovereignty and wisdom has been very supporting...I endeavoured to improve this our afflic - tion last Lord's day, from Psalm 46:10, "Be still and know that I am God." I principally dwelt upon two ideas, viz.:*
>
> *1. God has a sovereign right to dispose of us as he pleases.*
> *2. We ought to acquiesce in all that God does with us and to us.*[4]

## A TENACIOUS FAITH

Like Carey, Habakkuk's acquiescence was not mere resignation. This was not a prophet who had simply given up in his struggle with God. Rather, this was a prophet whom God had elevated so that he might be able to see the past, the present, and the future from the perspective of the kingdom of God.

Habakkuk purposed to cling to God through the storms which were about to be unleashed. This was not passive resignation, but rather tenacious faith. Habakkuk was going to trust that God would

---

4  Cited in *A Vision for Missions* by Tom Wells, The Banner of Truth Trust, Carlisle, PA, 1985, p. 135.

carry him through regardless of the calamities which were about to befall the prophet and his nation.

> *Though the fig tree does not bud and there are no grapes on the vines, though the olive crop fails and the fields produce no food, though there are no sheep in the pen and no cattle in the stalls, ... (Habakkuk 3:17)*

Habakkuk was anticipating some years of famine and hardship. He was unwilling to skirt the facts or to paint a rosy portrait of what was to come: there was an ugly future ahead, and Habakkuk knew it. In the midst of his unrelenting realism, he makes a remarkable stand:

> *... yet I will rejoice in the LORD, I will be joyful in God my Savior. (Habakkuk 3:18)*

How can he say this? Is Habakkuk in denial? How can he speak of joy when disaster is imminent? How can Habakkuk rejoice when his nation is about to be invaded by a fierce and relentless enemy?

In a sense, this is *the* challenge for all of us, the key to all of life: how do we live in fullness when the circumstances of life drain us? How can we experience on-going joy in the midst of life's discouragements? How can we smile when the pain is real? How can we live above the storms of life while at the same time remaining engaged in life itself? How are we to avoid *burnout* when we are confronted with disappointments, with hurts and with failed expec-tations?

## FINDING JOY IN THE MIDST OF PAIN

> *The Sovereign LORD is my strength; he makes my feet like the feet of a deer, he enables me to go on the heights. (Habakkuk 3:19)*

Although Habakkuk was trembling on the outside, inside he was discovering strength which simply had not previously existed. The Sovereign Lord had become his strength. At the outset of Habakkuk's journey, he wasn't convinced of the goodness of God's sovereignty. From his perspective, God's employment of Babylon as a means of judging His own people seemed like an unfair overreaction. Indeed, the sovereignty of God may appear to us to be a cruel or capricious thing. In fact, it is our only hope of not burning out in the ministry. Jonathan Edwards described his own struggle with the concept of God's sovereignty in his <u>Personal Narrative</u> and the way in which his changing perspective became a source of great comfort and joy.

> *From my childhood up, my mind had been wont to be full of objections against the doctrine of God's sovereignty....I have often since, not only had a conviction, but a delightful conviction. The doctrine of God's sovereignty has very often appeared, an exceeding pleasant, bright and sweet doctrine to me: and absolute sovereignty is what I love to ascribe to God. But my first conviction was not with this.* [5]

## How God's Sovereignty Affects Our Lives

When you, your family or your church are in crisis, how do you respond? Do you embrace the sovereign grace of God as your only hope? Do you see all of the events of your life, both the delightful ones and the destructive ones, as part of the sovereign working of God in your life and in the lives of those around you? Can you accept the disciplines of the Lord as gifts of grace to you? This is the way in which we avoid *burnout*—by seeing all of life and ministry as a

---

5 Cited in *A Jonathan Edwards Reader*, edited by John E. Smith, Harry S. Stout, and Kenneth P. Minkema, Yale University Press, New Haven, CT, 1995, p. 283.

direct expression of the sovereign grace of God in our lives. We must reject the notion that life is but a random series of unfolding events and embrace the full sovereignty of God. In this way, the Sovereign Lord becomes our strength and, as a result, we are able to live joyfully in spite of the traumas of life.

Does this really work or is this just spiritual talk, religious words which sound pious but which are not grounded in the here and now? Surely for Habakkuk these truths became a rock-solid reality. Undoubtedly there was a lengthy process involved. We might read the book of Habakkuk in ten or fifteen minutes, but in fact, the process Habakkuk went through may have lasted months or even years. Regardless of how long it took, he emerged as a different man. The way he viewed life, ministry, and himself was radically changed because he saw God more clearly. God recast Habakkuk's understanding of Himself as wiser, more engaged, more loving, more wrathful, more powerful, and more sovereign, indeed, a more accurate picture of the way He really is.

Habakkuk, as a prophet, and you and I as pastors or mission-aries, have an impossible task; we are to bring to people an accurate view of God—a God whom we barely understand ourselves! God is bigger, grander, and fuller than any of us realize, yet we are called as His spokesmen and are responsible to present Him to our people so that they might worship Him, obey Him and love Him. Who can bear this? If the most brilliant astrophysicist can only explain a minuscule portion of the universe, what hope have we to describe the One who holds the universe in the palm of His hand? Yet we must, for this is our lofty calling. Like Habakkuk, we must allow God to continuously expand our understanding of Himself.

Not only did God *grow* in Habakkuk's estimation, but simulta-neously, Habakkuk *shrank* in his own estimation of himself. The Lord reshaped Habakkuk's self-understanding and enabled him to see that he was less in control, less certain of what was truly best and less confident of knowing what God should or should not do. As a result, Habakkuk became acutely aware of his total depend - ency upon the Lord. This dependency became his freedom, en- abling him to rejoice even though he was caught up in a drama much larger than himself and to experience joy even though life sometimes had the appearance of being out of control. The Sover- eign Lord had become his strength.

## WHAT TRANSFORMED HABAKKUK?

Habakkuk came through his crisis of faith well, but he recognized that even his ability to respond in faith to the Sovereign Lord was a gift of grace. It was the Lord who enabled Habakkuk to go on the heights, who gave him feet like a deer, and who became his strength. The explanation was God and God alone.

What transformed this man from a state of confusion and despair to a place of hope and freedom? How did Habakkuk move through his disappointments and failed expectations to a place of joy and confident strength? How was the prophet able to grow from doubting God's goodness and wisdom to trusting in His unfailing love? How was Habakkuk able to rejoice even though the stalls were empty, the fields barren, and the vines without fruit? He was transformed by a vision of a Sovereign Lord reigning over all of His works. In that reality, Habakkuk was able to rest, confident that God would carry him through the most difficult circumstances.

God did a marvelous work in Habakkuk, the very work He desires for you and me. God desires to bring us from weariness to strength, from the depth of despair to the height of joy. Doesn't your soul hunger to rush swiftly upward with Habakkuk, to stand on top of that great mountain called "the Sovereign Lord"? It is only on this mountain that we may find protection from the scourge called *burnout*.

## REFLECTIONS, COMMITMENTS AND PRAYER

*Father, I confess that I often have a limited perspective on life. Forgive me when I have been overconfident and have insisted that my understanding was best and that my direction was the only way. You, Lord, know all things; You alone see what is best in the future. Enable me to rest in that truth, to "fit in" with what You are doing.*

*When the circumstances of life come crashing down on me, help me to see You in the midst of the difficulties. Help me to trust in Your sovereign goodness even when it appears that You are silent and distant. Give me the supernatural ability to rejoice even when I am disap - pointed with You or with others. Become my strength. Make my feet like the feet of a deer and enable me to go on the heights.*

*Simon, Simon, Satan has asked to sift you as wheat. But I have prayed for you, Simon, that your faith may not fail. And when you have turned back, strengthen your brothers.*

*Luke 22:31,32*

# 5

## *Peter: When We Disappoint Ourselves*

For many of us in the ministry, Peter is our favorite of all the apostles. We can identify with him so well! His impulsive, whole-hearted responses to the Lord, even when they set him up for deep failures, are a great encouragement. He leaps into deep water, he freely makes bold, sweeping statements, and he leaves everything and follows the Messiah. Peter experienced great "highs" in his life and ministry as well as terrible "lows."

Peter is not only an encouraging example for us; he is also a powerful model for God's protection against ministry *burnout*. From Peter, we learn about the battles with the enemy that take place in the mind. We learn about the transforming power of the Holy Spirit in the life of a man, and we learn that God is able to fulfill all of His will, even with weak people who come to Him with a whole heart.

## BUILDING THE WRONG KINGDOM

The apostle Peter likely shared a mindset that was very popular among God's people during that time; it was the expectation that the Messiah would be a political redeemer. When we put those fleshly expectations together with Peter's unrealistic images of himself, we have a fertile framework for Satan's deadly attacks and deceptions.

When the multitudes were responding to Christ in tremendous numbers, Jesus asked the disciples what the people were saying about Him.

> *Jesus and his disciples went on to the villages around Caesarea Philippi. On the way he asked them, "Who do people say I am?"* (Mark 8:27)

As Jesus continued, we can see that He had some degree of interest in how people saw Him, but He had a deep heart investment in the way His disciples saw Him. After listening to the perceptions of the multitudes who had experienced His healing power, deliverance from the bonds of Satan, and full meals from handfuls of bread and fish, He asked, "Who do you say I am?"

> *They replied, "Some say John the Baptist; others say Elijah; and still others, one of the prophets." "But what about you?" he asked. "Who do you say I am?" Peter answered, "You are the Christ."* (Mark 8:28,29)

It was Peter who cried out, "You are the Christ!" This teaching is within the context of the Lord's disciples having great difficulty seeing the reality of the Messiah in their midst. But the Holy Spirit opened Peter's eyes to see, and he responded with the strong affirmation that Jesus is, in fact, the Son of God.

After warning the disciples not to tell anyone about Him, Jesus began to build on Peter's confession that He is the Christ. He talked to His followers about the purpose of His coming as the Messiah. Jesus taught the disciples about His coming suffering, His rejection and His death.

> *He then began to teach them that the Son of Man must suffer many things and be rejected by the elders, chief priests and teachers of the law, and that he must be killed and after three days rise again. (Mark 8:31)*

How does Peter respond to this teaching? Does the one who just proclaimed that Jesus was God's anointed One, the Savior of His people, continue to affirm this further revelation of the person and purpose of Christ?

> *He spoke plainly about this, and Peter took him aside and began to rebuke him. (Mark 8:32)*

Peter does not affirm Jesus' message. In fact, right in the middle of His preaching, we can almost see Peter tugging on Jesus' sleeve and saying, "What are you talking about, Jesus? Why are you focusing on suffering, rejection and death? That is not what this is all about! We are going to defeat Rome. We are going to set up another kingdom. We are going to rule together. That is the purpose of your coming! What are you talking about?"

Peter had just proclaimed that Jesus was the Christ, but when Jesus began to reveal further what it meant to be the Christ, Peter could not see it. His eyes were blinded to the realities of the Messiah and to the eternal kingdom He would bring. Peter thought he had great hopes and dreams for ministry, but in reality his heart had become very small, shrunken to the size of his own images and expectations.

## THE BATTLES ARE AGAINST FORCES OF DARKNESS

Jesus then revealed to His disciple, and to us, the reality of Peter's battle and what was actually taking place in his mind and heart.

> *But when Jesus turned and looked at his disciples, he rebuked Peter. "Get behind me, Satan!" he said. "You do not have in mind the things of God, but the things of men." (Mark 8:33)*

We cannot imagine a stronger rebuke than Jesus' response to Peter. Our Lord confronts this beloved disciple as if Satan were speaking through him. Peter's mind has become filled up with the things of men. The hopes, dreams and plans of a temporal kingdom, and possibly his place of leadership in it, have consumed Peter's heart in such a way that his eyes have become blinded to the eternal kingdom that God will build through the death and resurrection of His Son. As Mark continues his narrative, Jesus also calls the disciples to lay down their lives.

Christ speaks to Peter as Satan and confronts him with what is in his mind. It is in this experience that we see the enemy's method of attack against the people of God. The battles for our personal lives, marriages, families and ministries are against the forces of darkness in the heavenly realms. They are not fought against flesh and blood. A belligerent church board, a congregation that lacks vision, or a divided people are not the enemy. Paul made this clear in his letter to the church at Ephesus.

> *Put on the full armor of God so that you can take your stand against the devil's schemes. For our struggle is not against flesh and blood, but against the rulers, against the authorities, against the powers of this dark world and against the spiritual forces of evil in the heavenly realms. (Ephesians 6:11,12)*

It would be wonderful if our battles were against flesh and blood! If that were true, our brilliance, our eloquence, our persua -

siveness and our personalities would be sufficient resources to take to the battles. However, since we are in warfare against the powers of wickedness in heavenly places, we need eternal resources with which to fight. Only God's armor will protect us here.

> *Therefore put on the full armor of God, so that when the day of evil comes, you may be able to stand your ground, and after you have done everything, to stand. Stand firm then, with the belt of truth buckled around your waist, with the breastplate of right-eousness in place ... (Ephesians 6:13,14)*

That is a wonderful promise for the people of God, and espe - cially for us who are on the front lines of the battles! We can stand, and stand firm! The first piece of God's armor for His warriors is the belt of truth. It is God's truth that will enable us to stand when our enemy is seeking to tear us down or even to stand in opposition to God's kingdom work, as he was with Peter.

Truth is God's first level of protection because Satan will work in our minds to steal away an understanding of what God is doing and how we might walk with Him in His eternal purposes. The truths of who God is, who our Father has made us to be in His Son, and the work of His kingdom to which God has called us will be the battle points. We see this same teaching set before the Corin - thian church by the apostle Paul.

> *For though we live in the world, we do not wage war as the world does. The weapons we fight with are not the weapons of the world. On the contrary, they have divine power to demolish strongholds. (2 Corinthians 10:3,4)*

Our Father has raised us up for warfare. We are in a terrible battle with those who have set themselves against Christ and His kingdom. God has called us to tear down the strongholds that Satan has built in the realms of this world and in the hearts and minds of people.

We see terrible strongholds everywhere we look in this world. We see the strongholds of political structures that enslave, poverty, sickness, and religious systems which bring no life, and materialism, rationalism, racism, and individualism. We also see strongholds of disobedience and personal rebellion against the Lord. How do we fight against enemies such as these?

Even though we are physically present in this world, Paul said that we do not wage war as the world does. We do not use the weapons of this system in our battles against the enemy. The power of armies and the strength of the will, as well as the brilliance of mind and eloquence of speech, are meaningless here. The weapons God gives destroy spiritual fortresses! Paul described these weapons as the knowledge of God and a heart of obedience.

*We demolish arguments and every pretension that sets itself up against the knowledge of God, and we take captive every thought to make it obedient to Christ. And we will be ready to punish every act of disobedience, once your obedience is complete. (2 Corinthians 10:5,6)*

God has called us to invade the darkness around us, tear down the strongholds of the enemy, and walk with God in the building of a kingdom which will never pass away. Our Father has given us four weapons for such warfare. One is prayer (Eph. 6:10-20) and another is worship (2 Chron. 20:1-23). Paul sets two other weapons before us here in 2 Corinthians 10, and neither of them is based on our own strength or abilities. We reject any resource that comes from us. Only proclaiming the truth of who God is and walking with a heart of obedience before Him will make any difference in these battles.

## OUR MINDS ARE THE BATTLEGROUND

The New International Version uses the word "arguments" in 2 Corinthians 10:5, and the New American Standard Bible translates it as "speculations." In that way the enemy comes to us as he seeks to steal away a heart of obedience. He wages war within our minds, leading us to "speculate" rather than to obey. The seeds of failure which can and will impact our life in Christ and ministry within the church begin with thoughts in the mind stimulated by the speculative wooing of Satan.

This is just what Peter was experiencing when he rejected Christ's commitment to follow His Father's leading into suffering, rejection and death. Satan was speaking another message into Peter's mind and heart. It was a message of self and of personal advancement; it called for political triumph rather than the cross. Satan came to Eve in the Garden of Eden with this same method of attack.

*Now the serpent was more crafty than any of the wild animals the LORD God had made. He said to the woman, "Did God really say, 'You must not eat from any tree in the garden'?"*
*(Genesis 3:1)*

The battle in the Garden of Eden was fought and lost on the basis of "What has God said?" Satan is slandering God's Word, His nature and His character before Eve. God had told Adam and Eve to eat freely of all the trees in the garden except the Tree of the Knowledge of Good and Evil, for the day that they ate of it, they would die (Gen. 2:16,17). Now Satan is causing Eve to speculate about the nature of a God who would withhold such good things from her. God had told them to eat freely of all the trees except one, and the Evil One says, "God won't let you eat from any tree." He is subtly building into Eve's mind questions about God's character. "He is not a good God, Eve. He holds back good things."

Satan was waging war against Eve's mind, and it was in her speculations and Adam's disobedience that the great tragedy of the Fall took place. We see this same strategy when God called Moses to be His deliverer of the enslaved Israelites in Egypt. When God was speaking to Moses, the enemy was right there, flooding his mind and heart with a myriad of "what if" questions. "Who am I that I should go to Pharaoh?...Suppose I go to the Israelites...What if they do not believe me?" (Exod. 3 & 4). Satan also came to Christ in the wilderness with this same strategy. "If you are the Son of God, tell these stones to become bread.... If you are the Son of God, throw yourself down" (Matt. 4:3-6). The enemy is seeking to cause Jesus to speculate about why God would allow Him to go hungry if He really was His Son, or why there is not more outward proof to the identity He holds in His heart.

We see this battle expressed in many ways today. People often walk out of our churches on Sunday mornings and say to the pastor, "You really gave me something to think about today." Of course, that is a valuable part of a larger process, but our enemy seeks to build into us a mindset that God gives us His Word for us to think about, as if our Father had some great eternal investment in expanding the insights of our minds. His desire is to transform our hearts, our relationships, our motives, and values, our passions and priorities. When God speaks to us about our attitudes toward our marriage partners, our finances, our time, money or sexual desires, we may well respond with "what if" questions or say, "Yes...if, or yes...but, or yes...when." It is in that kind of speculation that Satan specializes in the battles of our minds.

I have often seen churches whose congregations are in the midst of pain and division, and people on all sides are convinced that they are "right." Satan does not care at all who is right. His desire is the pain, the division and the lost love and unity which reveal the reality of Christ in our midst. In this process, our enemy will slander brothers and sisters in one another's minds, stimulating ungodly attitudes and responses which result in the deadly fruit of destruc - tion which He truly desires. These are the speculations which today undermine the life of the church.

It is the war in the mind that the enemy fights so well, and that is why we must constantly guard our hearts and our minds with the "belt of truth." Only the truth about God and the words that He speaks will guard us in these subtle attacks from the enemy. Look at the way in which Paul follows his call to proclaim the knowledge of God and to take every thought captive to obedience in his message to the Corinthians.

*I hope you will put up with a little of my foolishness; but you are already doing that. I am jealous for you with a godly jealousy. I promised you to one husband, to Christ, so that I might present you as a pure virgin to him. (2 Corinthians 11:1,2)*

Paul guarded his people with a "godly jealousy." His desire was to present them pure before the Lord. What battles would Paul and God's people have to face in that process?

*But I am afraid that just as Eve was deceived by the serpent's cunning, your minds may somehow be led astray from your sincere and pure devotion to Christ. (2 Corinthians 11:3)*

The battle for our lives in Christ and our ministries is fought primarily in our minds and is won or lost as we either bring every thought captive to obedience, or do not. Those of us in ministry are primary targets of Satan's subtle attacks concerning God's good - ness, His character and His promises. When things are not going well, the enemy will be right there slandering our good and glorious God in our minds, raising questions about our identity in Christ, and questioning God's call in our lives, His commitments to us and His care for us along the way.

## FAILED EXPECTATIONS

One of my most treasured friends over the years is also one of the greatest preachers I have ever heard. Throughout his seminary training and early service to the Lord, he was one of the "rising stars" for the Church in the eyes of everyone who heard him. We all knew that he would have an incredibly successful ministry, as he was not only an unusually gifted teacher but had the good looks and the winning personality to go with it all.

My friend also knew that within a few years, he would have one of the largest churches in the area. But it never happened. In fact, he is no longer in the pastoral ministry. God never met his expectations, and I believe that the enemy built into him a slow, subtle dissatisfaction with not only his church and his elders, but also with his finances, his wife, and even with God. He finally gave up. His marriage and his pastorate were both lost. It broke my heart to see him hurt like that and his gifts and ministry to be lost to the Church, if only for a time. However, I am convinced of his sincere desire to serve the Lord, and I believe that God is not finished with him yet. Our Father is still in the process with him as he was with Peter, and God will bring him through this. God's glory will be seen on the other side of these difficult days.

I believe in his mind my friend succumbed to Satan's slandering of God and others. As a church, we have become increasingly less diligent, less disciplined, and less convinced that the renewing of our minds is a needed daily pursuit. We are less committed to the transforming process of submitting our minds and hearts to the work of God's Holy Spirit through the Scriptures. To the extent we are failing in this process, we are not only being conformed to this world, but we are, with the enemy, sowing the seeds that fuel *burnout* in our ministries, and we will lose heart along the way.

We see this very battle being fought in Peter's mind and heart, as Satan sought to destroy him as a person and a minister. Previously we saw Peter's expectations concerning God's kingdom that got him into trouble, but his expectations concerning himself made him very vulnerable as well. Just like my friend who was worn down by the images of success the enemy had planted in his mind, Peter's illusions about himself were part of the enemy's strategy.

In the last hours that Christ spent with His disciples before He went to the cross, He washed their feet and taught them to serve one another. He then told them that He would be going away and that they could not go with Him. Peter responded in this way:

*Peter asked, "Lord, why can't I follow you now? I will lay down my life for you." (John 13:37)*

This is vintage Peter! Images of himself blown clearly out of proportion, making commitments with his mouth that his flesh could not fulfill. Again, Christ spoke confrontively about what would take place in the next few hours.

*Then Jesus answered, "Will you really lay down your life for me? I tell you the truth, before the rooster crows, you will disown me three times!" (John 13:38)*

## SATAN IS GOD'S TOOL

As the apostle Luke relates this same incident, he reveals the depth of the battle that is actually taking place in Peter's mind and heart. Satan is seeking Peter's destruction!

*"Simon, Simon, Satan has asked to sift you as wheat. But I have prayed for you, Simon, that your faith may not fail. And when you have turned back, strengthen your brothers." (Luke 22:31,32)*

This is an amazingly clear picture not only of God's sovereignty over evil, but the way in which He uses Satan to fulfill His purposes in the lives and ministries of His people. Satan desired to separate Peter from his faith like the chaff is separated from the grain in the threshing process, but Jesus' promise of His presence with Peter in the midst of this terrible battle would be all of his hope. The assurance that he would not be destroyed but further prepared for ministry in this experience would be Peter's only basis for confi - dence.

What have been the "sifting experiences" of your life? In what circumstances has Satan desired to destroy you and remove you from ministry? How has God used these experiences to further prepare you for the work to which He has called you?

How does Peter respond to Christ's ministry? Does He fall at Jesus' feet with worship, praise and thanksgiving flowing from his heart? No, we hear even more fleshly boasts!

*But he replied, "Lord, I am ready to go with you to prison and to death." (Luke 22:33)*

Rather than worshiping Christ for His faithful promises and His loving commitments, Peter's view of himself in the battle is totally out of proportion. What a setup from the enemy! We can almost hear Peter saying, "Jesus, you don't realize who you are talking to! This is not one of those weak disciples; this is Peter! When you are alone and afraid, you need only to remember that I will be there for you. I am going with you all the way, even if it costs me my life!"

Jesus confronted Peter with the reality of his circumstances and the depth of this battle.

*Jesus answered, "I tell you, Peter, before the rooster crows today, you will deny three times that you know me." (Luke 22:34)*

Peter was surely sincere when he made these commitments, but in his own strength he was unable to fulfill his promises. In fact, he wasn't even able to tell the young woman who was serving at the high priest's home that he belonged to Jesus. He cursed, he swore, and he denied any knowledge of Jesus. He heard the cock crow, looked up into the eyes of Jesus, went out and wept bitterly.

The guilt, the shame and the failure of this experience overwhelmed Peter's heart. His confusion and the fact that he had failed to measure up to his own expectations dealt such a blow to him that his hopes for the ministry were destroyed. He had burned out and lost heart. Only God's presence in the battle with him and the truth that the Father's process of development was not yet complete would bring Peter to the fruitful ministry God had prepared for him from the foundation of the world.

## FROM THE FISHERMAN TO THE SHEPHERD

How did God bring Peter to the place of fruitful ministry after such great overwhelming failure and loss of heart? We see in His faithful process of healing and commissioning of Peter a reminder that God will use those whom He has chosen, just as we saw with Moses, Jeremiah and Ezekiel, and He will provide His keeping grace along the way.

Peter had gone back to fishing. Though it is very difficult to go back to what one was, on this particular morning Peter and some of the other disciples had fished all night but had caught nothing. With Jesus' instructions to put the net on the other side of the boat, they brought in a huge catch. Jesus fixed breakfast for the disciples and then talked personally with Peter.

As far as we know, this was the first time Jesus and Peter had talked together personally since that terrible night when Peter denied Christ. I think Peter had given a great deal of thought to what Jesus would say to him when they discussed his failure. In fact, I think Peter (with the enemy's voice behind it) "played the tape" over and over in his mind. Possibly in the context of his guilt and shame, he felt that Jesus would say, "Peter, I want you to know that I understand what happened that night. I know that you were sincere in your commitments, but in the great pressure of the circumstances and the fear in your heart, you were not able to follow through with your promises. You need to know that I have forgiven you, Peter. I still love you. However, as far as the work of the kingdom is concerned, I'm afraid it will not work out the way we had hoped. The work of the kingdom is so eternally significant that I need to surround myself with strong men whom I can trust in any situation. I can't always be thinking, 'What is Peter going to do? What is Peter going to say when the heat gets turned up high again?' I still love you, Peter, and we will always be friends, but as far as the ministry of building my Church, that will not work out as we had hoped."

With all of my heart, I believe Peter felt that Jesus would speak to him in that way. Let's look at that conversation and see something of God's gracious ministry to Peter in the midst of his failure.

> *When they had finished eating, Jesus said to Simon Peter, "Simon son of John, do you truly love me more than these?" "Yes, Lord," he said, "you know that I love you." Jesus said, "Feed my lambs." (John 21:15)*

Perhaps the question, "Do you truly love me more than these?" has to do with the comparison of Peter's love for Christ with that of the other disciples. As you well know, Jesus is using one word for "love" and Peter responds with another. Jesus asks Peter, "Do you find within yourself the capacity to give yourself for me?", using the word for God's commitment love, which is expressed in a heart of giving. I am sure that Peter thought to himself, "I am not going to overstate my commitment again!" so he responds, "Lord, you know I have affection for you."

Does Jesus respond to Peter by saying, "I was just checking to see what was there, Peter. If this is all the love you have for me, that is the end of this conversation."? No, our Lord meets Peter where he is and commissions him! "Feed my lambs!"

> *Again Jesus said, "Simon son of John, do you truly love me?" He answered, "Yes, Lord, you know that I love you." Jesus said, "Take care of my sheep." The third time he said to him, "Simon son of John, do you love me?" Peter was hurt because Jesus asked him the third time, "Do you love me?" He said, "Lord, you know all things; you know that I love you." Jesus said, "Feed my sheep." (John 21:16,17)*

Again, Christ asked Peter the same question and received the same answer. Once again Peter receives a commissioning from his Savior—"Take care of my sheep." The third time, Jesus changed his word for "love" to Peter's. "Peter, do you have affection for me?" Christ commissioned him once again. "Feed my sheep."

## GOD KEEPS HIS OWN BY HIS GRACE

There is no question in my mind that Peter never would have been used of God so powerfully in the building of His Church apart from Jesus' intimate, compassionate, loving work of healing, restoration and commissioning. This is God's way with us, too. I have been watching God heal and restore the brother I told you about earlier. In the environment of his repentance and our Lord's great mercy, his heart was not destroyed, and God is commissioning him anew. Even though he is not in the "pastoral ministry," he is involved in several Bible studies and discipleship ministries. God has kept his heart by His grace, just as He did with Peter.

Then the Son of God amazingly told Peter how he would die.

*"I tell you the truth, when you were younger you dressed yourself and went where you wanted; but when you are old you will stretch out your hands, and someone else will dress you and lead you where you do not want to go." Jesus said this to indicate the kind of death by which Peter would glorify God. Then he said to him, "Follow me!" (John 21:18,19)*

Why would Jesus tell Peter at this point how he would die? What kind of love would it take for Peter to be obedient to Christ's command to follow Him, knowing that this obedience would cost him his life? Only God's deep, giving love would enable Peter to follow his Lord in such a costly way. Jesus is saying to him, "I know the capacity that you have to give yourself for me because I am putting that into your heart!" Christ is teaching Peter to see himself through the eyes of God!

I like the rest of the story, too.

*Peter turned and saw that the disciple whom Jesus loved was following them. (This was the one who had leaned back against Jesus at the supper and had said, "Lord, who is going to betray you?") When Peter saw him, he asked, "Lord, what about him?" Jesus answered, "If I want him to remain alive until I return, what is that to you? You must follow me." (John 21:20-22)*

How does Peter respond to his Lord's loving ministry of resto - ration? Do we see worship, praise and thanksgiving? No, Peter happened to see John walking by and said, "What about him?" We can almost hear Jesus replying, "Peter, you have enough to concern yourself with in your own relationship to me. Let me take care of John, and you follow me!"

In many ways, Peter never really changed. He remained a weak, impulsive man with the tendency to say the wrong thing at the wrong time. Yet, God fulfilled all of His will in Peter, as He will with weak people like you and me when we come before Him with a whole heart.

Just as we saw with Elijah, God took the initiative and came to Peter when Peter had given up. And how did He come? With a powerful wind that could shatter rock? With an earthquake that would shake him into reality or a fire that could consume him? No, Jesus came with the gentle whisper, "Peter...do you love me? Peter...do you love me? Peter...do you love me?" And that is the way He will come to you and me when we have failed or lost heart and strength.

Peter was confused from the very beginning of Jesus' call in his life. He thought this was all about building a kingdom. Now he was learning that God's call was first to the building of a love relation- ship. Sometimes we get confused as well, and we look at our ministries as building kingdoms, and Jesus is whispering to us over and over again, "Do you love me?...Do you love me?"

## EMPTYING AND FILLING

What was the means by which God brought Peter, a man who bore great weaknesses and failures, to a place of power and fruitfulness in ministry? We see in Peter not only God's keeping grace but an amazing process of emptying and filling as God prepared him for the work of His Church. After Christ was raised from the dead, He appeared before the disciples for a period of forty days. Just before His ascension, He spoke these words.

> On one occasion, while he was eating with them, he gave them this command: "Do not leave Jerusalem, but wait for the gift my Father promised, which you have heard me speak about. For John baptized with water, but in a few days you will be baptized with the Holy Spirit." (Acts 1:4,5)

The apostles went back to Jerusalem in obedience to the Lord's command and returned to the room where they were staying, and they waited. It was during this time that, under Peter's leadership, they chose Matthias to take Judas' place as an apostle. Luke describes for us how they spent those days.

> *They all joined together constantly in prayer, along with the women and Mary the mother of Jesus, and with his brothers. (Acts 1:14)*

Jesus had not told the apostles and disciples how long it would be before the coming of the Holy Spirit. He did say "in a few days," but we know that a "few days" to God can be many days to us! We know now that it was a period of ten days that they waited and prayed.

Wouldn't it have been understandable if, after five or six days of prayer, one of the apostles had stood up and said, "Brothers and sisters, we have just been given a great commission from our Lord. We are to take the gospel to Jerusalem, to Judea, to Samaria, and to the whole world. How can we most effectively fulfill this commission? Who are the best speakers in the group? Why don't you go over into that corner and talk about the message? Who are the best organizers? Why don't you meet over here and discuss the best methods to get the message out? Who are the best at handling the finances? Who should go out to the cities and towns before the speakers arrive and let them know that the message is coming?

It would have made complete sense if they had divided into committees, but they did not. They waited and they prayed. This was God's emptying process before His filling process. The disciples and the apostles were being emptied of their own plans, hopes, dreams, and any confidence in themselves and their abilities. We can see this taking place in Peter's heart—this man who always had an answer for everything and whose eyes were filled up with his dreams for a new kingdom and his place of prominence in it.

> *When the day of Pentecost came, they were all together in one place. Suddenly a sound like the blowing of a violent wind came*

*from heaven and filled the whole house where they were sitting. (Acts 2:1,2)*

## FILLED WITH THE HOLY SPIRIT

This was the environment into which the Holy Spirit came! A group of men and women who had been taught by their Lord, had witnessed His resurrection, and had been emptied of themselves, their resources, their hopes and their dreams. We are very much like them. How can we be filled without first being emptied?

*They saw what seemed to be tongues of fire that separated and came to rest on each of them. All of them were filled with the Holy Spirit and began to speak in other tongues as the Spirit enabled them. (Acts 2:3,4)*

When all those who had gathered there heard the believers speaking in other tongues, the people thought they were drunk, but Peter stood and addressed the multitudes.

*Then Peter stood up with the Eleven, raised his voice and addressed the crowd: "Fellow Jews and all of you who live in Jerusalem, let me explain this to you; listen carefully to what I say. These men are not drunk, as you suppose. It's only nine in the morning! No, this is what was spoken by the prophet Joel:...* *(Acts 2:14-16)*

It was this weak, impulsive man, the one that we all thought would never learn, whom God raised up as His messenger that day. Peter's sermon was the Word of God. He brought the Scriptures to the people that day with such authority that three thousand were added to God's Church. What was it that transformed Peter? How did he go from a weak, fleshly, confused man who could only see God in light of his own dreams and desires, to an apostle of power and authority? It was the filling of God's Holy Spirit that trans-formed Peter, as well as all of the other apostles!

We see God's wonderful and faithful process in Peter's life, a process that brought him to a place of power and fruitfulness. This is also God's process for you and me. It could be that you are in the same place that Peter was after his great failure, feeling that there is little hope that God would ever use you again, or that you would be sentenced to God's "second best" for the rest of your life and ministry. Perhaps you, too, have lived with illusions of all that you would do for God, but those dreams have not been fulfilled. Maybe you are at the same place as my friend who lost heart when his expectations for God and for himself were not met.

We have a God who fulfills all of His will in those whom He chooses for ministry. By His grace He keeps those whom He raises up for His glorious, eternal purposes. If you are struggling now, you need to be reminded that God is not finished with you yet. He will keep you, too, by His grace. He will empty you and fill you with His Holy Spirit. As you draw on the resources of God's Spirit, the ministry to which you are called will be marked by God's fruitful - ness and power, just as Peter's was. With our great God, there is always the hope and confidence that the best days of ministry are yet ahead, no matter where we have been! That is the significance of His keeping grace.

## REFLECTIONS, COMMITMENTS AND PRAYER

*"Lord, I know that I have failed You, just as Peter failed You. I, too, am weak, and I so often see those things that enhance me and the kingdom that I desire to build. I have been so vulnerable to Satan's battle in my mind, and I pray that You will enable me today to take every thought captive in my obedience to Christ. Would You continue to keep me by Your grace, even as my enemy would destroy me, and use him as a tool in Your hands to make me the person You desire me to be for Your glory? Give me the*

*grace to see myself through Your eyes, even as You did Peter when You restored him. Please empty me of my own plans and dreams as You did the disciples in that upper room, and fill me with the power of your Holy Spirit for the great work that You have set before me in the building of Your Church."*

*Stop judging by mere appearances, and make a right judgment.*

*John 7:24*

# 6

## *Jesus: When the Spotlight Seduces Us*

Life in the spotlight is one of the most treacherous places of all. The temptations of a public ministry and the deceptions which we can so easily absorb make the pastoral ministry especially dangerous. The dangers are multiple and subtle. The most obvious temptation is in the area of our motivations: doing and saying things in order to boost our image or to curry favor. Each of us in public ministry is aware of this danger, yet it continues to be an insidious enemy. One Sunday morning we may preach with the purest of motives, yet that evening find our hearts longing for the approval of our audience. The temptations to highlight our own learning, insight, righteousness, or humility(!) constantly barrage us. As professional communicators, some of us have learned well the art of maintaining a well-crafted image.

The dangers of public ministry make us especially susceptible to *burnout*. When ministry becomes a means to meet our own personal needs, we find a host of new pressures upon us. The pressure to perform can be overwhelming. Our own expectations for personal success can crush us. Our efforts to cover ourselves and to hide our inadequacies and "secrets" can be exhausting. Our desires to please other people can drain us of a sense of integrity. When we focus on externals, we become more concerned with appearances and less with substance. Ministry has enough genuine, inherent pressures in itself. *Burnout* becomes inevitable if we succumb to these additional pressures in an effort to try to satisfy our needs for approval and recognition.

Jesus faced the powerful temptations inherent to public ministry. He, too, was tempted to live the life of a celebrity preacher. Jesus surely was tempted to soften the truth, to focus on appearances, to take short cuts. How did Jesus deal with His need of approval? How was Jesus able to ignore the constant chorus of voices, both within and without, which beckoned Him to build a movement, an image, and a reputation? How did Jesus manage to travel through Vanity Fair without succumbing to its evocative call? Fortunately, the Scriptures show us the way.

In this chapter we will learn from Jesus the dangers of public ministry: seeking approval in the wrong places, defending ourselves, building our personal reputations, focusing on appearances rather than substance, and living in a "performance" mode. We will discover that our public ministry is to flow out of a security rooted in our Father's acceptance, a heart that is vulnerable and humble, and a sense of God's timing and agenda.

## THE DANGER OF PERFORMANCE

Jesus' first public act as an adult was His baptism by John. What a glorious experience for Jesus as both the Father and the Spirit affirmed Him before John and the people!

132

*When all the people were being baptized, Jesus was baptized too. And as he was praying, heaven was opened and the Holy Spirit descended on him in bodily form like a dove. And a voice came from heaven: "You are my Son, whom I love; with you I am well pleased." (Luke 3:21,22)*

Immediately after His baptism, Jesus stepped out of the Jordan River, ready to begin His ministry.

*Jesus, full of the Holy Spirit, returned from the Jordan and was led by the Spirit in the desert, where for forty days he was tempted by the devil.... (Luke 4:1,2)*

What a curious beginning! Jesus is full of the Holy Spirit; He's ready to go! Yet, God sends Him, not among the crowds, but into the desert. Whenever I have had an exciting personal encounter with the Lord, I want to tell someone about it. I want to step up to the pulpit! Instead, the Spirit leads Jesus into the wilderness. Jesus' sense of time and place flows from His relationship with His Father. Jesus moved in and out of public ministry through the direction of the Holy Spirit in His life. We will return shortly to this idea and discover that it is a way of life for Jesus, a pattern that protected Him from *burnout*.

The three well-known temptations of Jesus follow in Luke's account. Each offers Jesus an opportunity to prove Himself and to validate His ministry. They are all from the pit of hell.

*The devil said to him, "If you are the Son of God, tell this stone to become bread." (Luke 4:3)*

Satan's very first word to Jesus is loaded. "If" is a clever dagger with two deadly edges. On one hand, it raises doubt about the Father's love, affirmation, and veracity. "Are you really God's Son? Is this how He treats His Son, letting Him practically starve to death? What are you doing in this God-forsaken wilderness?" The experience at the Jordan river must have seemed light years away by now. Those precious words, "You are my Son," must have sounded like a distant echo in Jesus' ears. Just as with Eve, Satan tries to entice Jesus to doubt what His Father had said.

The other edge of the dagger is this: "Prove it, Jesus. Show me." Satan has slyly attempted to force Jesus into a performance mode. He has questioned Jesus' identity and challenged Him to defend Himself.

How often do we feel this compulsion to defend ourselves? We agonize if we sense that people misunderstand us. We want to be sure our people know how hard we work and how many hours we really put in. We are tempted to let others know how much we study or pray or visit. We may feel pressure at our pastors' fellowship to put a positive spin on our ministry, using the "best" numbers available for attendance, giving or baptisms. The more that our personal sense of value is performance-based, the more vulnerable we become to this temptation from our enemy.

## THE DANGER OF SHORT CUTS

*The devil led him up to a high place and showed him in an instant all the kingdoms of the world. And he said to him, "I will give you all their authority and splendor, for it has been given to me, and I can give it to anyone I want to. So if you worship me, it will all be yours." (Luke 4:5-7)*

Satan continues to question God's goodness to His Son. "Is He withholding from you the kingdoms of the world? Ha! Ha! He's given them to me!" He also questions the Father's timing. Satan knows that all the authority and splendor of the kingdoms of the world ultimately belong to Jesus. Perhaps Satan is offering Jesus a short cut, a way to avoid the cross: instant kingship, and glory without the pain. Jesus can have it all, now!

However, Jesus is unwilling to short cut the process since the timing is just as important as the goal. In North America, we tend to be goal-oriented. For many of us, the process is simply a bothersome prelude to the end product. Our culture is increasingly oriented toward immediate relief and instant gratification. In contrast, while God has glorious goals in mind for us, He is just as much concerned with the process. To Him, the means are as critical as the end.

For Jesus, suffering was an essential part of the process. For us, suffering and failure are critical components of what God is doing in and through us. Our public ministry has its glories, but the furnace of life is where we learn the lessons that make the message connect with the lives of our people. It is in our weakness that the power of God is manifested. Vulnerable, honest preaching resounds in the pews. We are indeed the children of glory, but first we must become "the people of the process." How do we avoid *burnout*? We recognize that ministry will be fraught with difficulty and failure and that by the grace of God the accompanying pain, rather than weakening our ministries, can actually empower our ministries.

We may take shortcuts in the ministry by avoiding certain difficult situations or people. Perhaps we rely on our knowledge and communication skills instead of doing the sometimes tedious work of study. We may forgo our "heart preparation" of prayer. Over the long run these short cuts will enfeeble our ministries and cause us to unduly rely on our own resources, which, when depleted, may well result in *burnout.*

## THE DANGER OF THE SPOTLIGHT

Satan, failing to entrap Jesus in the dangers of performance and instant success, circles around and tries again. His third temptation of Jesus also begins with a taunting "if." He dangles before the Lord another, more subtle short cut. Perhaps Jesus will "jump start" His ministry with a powerful and visible demonstration of power.

> *The devil led him to Jerusalem and had him stand on the highest point of the temple. "If you are the Son of God," he said, "throw yourself down from here. For it is written: 'He will command his angels concerning you to guard you carefully; they will lift you up in their hands, so that you will not strike your foot against a stone.'" (Luke 4:9-11)*

What a fantastic way this would be for Jesus to begin His ministry—a full swoon off the temple pinnacle in full view of the worshipers in the temple courts below. Can you imagine the impact if, while Jesus was free falling, a legion of angels were to soar from the clouds and sweep in to catch Him just a split second before He hit the ground? Talk about dramatic! Let's see Cecil B. DeMille match that! The "ohhs" and "ahhs" would reverberate for miles around.

Jesus said "no" to this temptation. To "cater to the crowds" in Jerusalem would violate his relationship with His most "significant Other," His Father. Jesus refused to test or challenge God, for this would be the very opposite of our Lord's lifelong intention. To accept Satan's offer would be to contradict the Father's way; it would be to choose a lesser plan. Jesus chose the Father's way, a way which did not begin in Jerusalem on the pinnacle overlooking the Temple mount. Rather, it began in the wilderness, in arid, lonely places far from the glare of the spotlight.

## WORKING BEHIND THE SCENES

Jesus recognized the dangers of prominence. Whenever possible, He avoided drawing attention to Himself or elevating His own status and reputation. He preferred to live and work behind the scenes, touching the broken lives of ordinary people. For Jesus, the fame and glory were only distractions.

Have you ever wondered why Jesus commanded both demons and people not to tell others who He was? In many ways such an attitude is counterintuitive. We know that the Son of God desires all men to be saved and to come to a knowledge of the truth (I Tim. 2:4). Why would He often veil His light?

Matthew records the healing of a man with leprosy (8:1-4), two blind men (9:27-31), and a large number of sick (12:15-17). After each of these incidents, Jesus "warned them not to tell who he was" (12:16). In the gospel of Mark, after Jesus healed Jairus' dead daughter, He "gave strict orders not to let anyone know about this" (5:21-43). He wasn't being modest, He really did not want people talking about this miracle. Later in Mark, Jesus gave a similar command to the friends of a deaf and dumb man whom he had graciously healed (7:31-37).

This doesn't sound exactly like a master plan for evangelism: "Don't tell anyone!" What is this obsession with secrecy? Why would the Son of Man not welcome the free publicity, the word-of-mouth, the good will which would surely flow out of these incidents? All of the examples cited occurred during Jesus' so-called public minis - try. So what is the problem?

Matthew gives us insight into Jesus' rationale. After a time of healing many people, Jesus warned those who were healed to not tell who he was. Matthew goes on to explain that this was "to fulfill what was spoken through the prophet Isaiah."

Matthew then quotes part of a messianic "Servant Song" from Isaiah 42.

*"Here is my servant whom I have chosen, the one I love, in whom I delight; I will put my Spirit on him, and he will proclaim justice to the nations. He will not quarrel or cry out; no one will hear his*

*voice in the streets. A bruised reed he will not break, and a smoldering wick he will not snuff out, till he leads justice to victory. In his name the nations will put their hope."* (Matthew 12:18-21)

## LIVING AN UNDERSTATED LIFE

Why does Matthew evoke the picture of the chosen Servant of the Lord who brings justice and hope to the nations? He clearly believed that the point was self-evident, that the *manner* in which this international messianic ministry would be conducted would be unassuming, understated, and gentle. The Servant of Isaiah reminds Matthew of Jesus in that the profound ministry of the Servant/Messiah involved a quiet process. Paradoxically, the One who will become the hope of the nations refuses to draw attention to Himself; rather, He will be a quiet, humble King. He will not despise the small, the broken, or the dying things. What graphic images Isaiah portrays: the Servant bending down to cradle a bruised reed which no one else would even notice, the Victorious One shielding a flickering wick which is about to be extinguished.

Clem Bilhorn is a man who ministers in an understated way. He has served as an associate pastor for almost his entire ministry. (He has also served ably as my father-in-law for a briefer period of time!) However, it is his capacity as an unassuming pastor that I find so striking. Clem embodies Matthew's description of the servant of the Lord; he hates being the center of attention. (He recently refused to buy an attractive red van because it would draw too much attention; the nondescript beige van would do just fine.)

If Clem knew that I was writing these words, he would beg me to stop, yet he combines an aversion to recognition with a servant's heart. He has spent his life ministering behind the scenes, often to unlovely people. He has often been the one at church helping people who walk in off the street and who may be "down on their luck."

He is the one people call in the middle of the night to help jump-start a stalled car. He is a man who has driven three hours round trip Saturday after Saturday to visit a ward of the state in one of Illinois' mental health hospitals. He has served countless hundreds of people over the years; he has led dozens and dozens of them to a saving knowledge of Jesus. You will never hear him "quarrel or cry out" because he is too busy tending to bruised reeds and smoldering wicks. Clem has learned well how to follow Jesus down the side roads and among the common people. In those unimpressive places, he has rarely found prominence, but in him, people have recognized Jesus.

Think about the ministry opportunities which come your way. We are tempted to say "yes" to those opportunities which have the highest profile. What if Promise Keepers were to invite you to speak at one of its huge gatherings? Would you have to stop and pray about it? Wouldn't you be tempted to jump at that opportunity immediately? If, on the other hand, a small, struggling church invites you to speak on a Wednesday evening, how are you tempted to respond? Aren't you tempted to say "no," before even consulting the Lord? I am. The spotlight caters to our flesh. We assume that bigger is better and therefore "of the Lord." Our flesh hurries onto the stage; it abhors anonymity and loves applause. May we resist the overpowering call of our flesh to the spotlight.

## THE DANGER OF AN IMAGE

As public figures you and I are vulnerable to the lure of the crowds. We have felt the temptations to enhance our public personage. Perhaps we are not as overt as our secular contemporaries, but the temptations are still there. We live in the midst of a cultural impulse which encourages, even demands, that we tend to our image.

The temptation for us to focus on appearances is strong. It is almost impossible for us not to be tainted with this worldly perspective for our culture is consumed with image. In a series of television commercials, tennis star André Agassi tells us, "Image is everything." Our public figures massage and contour their images according to their own devices. We see it emanating across our country, from Hollywood to Washington, D.C. to New York. Actors and actresses have always had their publicists; now even politicians employ "handlers" as well as "spin-meisters." Television newscasts are hopelessly enchanted with powerful and evocative images rather than reasoned and thoughtful analysis.

When Jesus began His public ministry at Nazareth, He came with good initial "press"—even without a public relations firm! During His first recorded sermon, people thought Jesus was great.

> *All spoke well of him and were amazed at the gracious words that came from his lips. "Isn't this Joseph's son?" they asked. (Luke 4:22)*

However, as Jesus preached the Word of God in the power of the Holy Spirit, some took great offense at Him, to the point in which they became furious with Him.

> *They got up, drove him out of the town, and took him to the brow of the hill on which the town was built, in order to throw him down the cliff. (Luke 4:29)*

Jesus did not preach to win friends and influence people. He unflinchingly refused to focus on His own reputation and standing. Jesus was unconcerned with what others thought, and focused entirely on the ministry and the message which His Father had given Him. If He had focused on public opinion, Jesus would have had to expend inordinate amounts of time and energy to fulfill lesser goals than those to which His Father had called Him. Jesus lived and ministered with one great goal: to please His Father.

Sometimes our desperate needs for the approval of others run deep and extend tentacles far below our field of vision. We recognize the most obvious dangers when the temptation comes in its most bald, grotesque expression. Most of us in ministry have seen and felt, but have refused to "buy into" the celebrity orientation of ministry with its focus on externals and its emphasis on "the show." We know that that road ends in death. Our problem arises not from a wholesale capitulation to this temptation, but rather from an acquiescence to its more subtle manifestations. In order to win approval or avoid disapproval, we may be tempted to "enhance" our stories, to soften a hard truth, to hide a personal fault, to tout our experience, to avoid a broken person, to desire a more promi - nent role, to highlight our education, or to please others rather than God.

We have the capacity to contour our public image in order to impress an audience. We know how to communicate well and are very vulnerable at this point. May God enable us as pastors and leaders to teach and preach with genuine humility and purity of heart. May He grace us to be vulnerable with our weaknesses and sins so that our people will become free from the pressures to maintain an image.

May we, like Jesus, learn to teach and preach to an audience of One.

## THE DANGER OF SUCCESS

*After this, Jesus went around in Galilee, purposely staying away from Judea because the Jews there were waiting to take his life. (John 7:1)*

Jesus found contentment and fulfillment ministering in the backwaters of Galilee, far from the cosmopolitan crowds of Jeru - salem and Judea. He knew the grave dangers of public ministry and avoided unnecessary danger, not out of fear, but out of wisdom. Jesus' family, however, had greater plans for him.

> *But when the Jewish Feast of Tabernacles was near, Jesus' brothers said to him, "You ought to leave here and go to Judea, so that your disciples may see the miracles you do. No one who wants to become a public figure acts in secret. Since you are doing these things, show yourself to the world." (John 7:2-4)*

The Feast of the Tabernacles was one of the three great pilgrim - age festivals of the Jewish year. Jerusalem was the one and only place to celebrate the feast. It was a "must" on the Israelite religious and social calendar; in fact, every male was required to be in attendance.

What a perfect time and place for Jesus to launch His ministry. Although He had been ministering in Galilee for about two years, the ministry still had a parochial feel to it. Nazareth and Capernaum were hardly the places from which to establish a significant ministry. After two years, one would think that the Son of God would have a considerably larger ministry!

Perhaps Jesus needed some marketing advice. His brothers were clearly impressed by what they saw Jesus doing. The miracles had been noteworthy and beyond anything they could have imagined. They simply didn't understand why Jesus would continue to work in relative obscurity when Judea was a wide-open market opportunity just a few miles south.

When I studied marketing, one simple device which summa - rized marketing essentials was the "Four Ps" of the marketing mix: promotion, price, placement, and product. Jesus was a great "product" and you couldn't beat the price (free!) However, His placement and promotional efforts were rather dismal.

"Show yourself to the world," the brothers urged. "Become a public figure, a man of standing, a celebrity." We too have heard these urgings! Well-meaning people tell us to develop a cassette ministry, or even better, a radio ministry. Perhaps we could move into a video ministry, or best of all, television! Perhaps we have thought to ourselves that our church really wasn't equal to our capacities. A more substantial ministry in a larger town would be much more desirable. There we might finally be discovered.

The pressures to create a "successful" ministry can be enormous and lead to *burnout*. Jesus refused to define *success* by the number of His followers or by the weight of His reputation. Instead, He defined *success* as faithfully doing His Father's work when and where His Father directed.

> *You go to the Feast. I am not yet going up to this Feast, because for me the right time has not yet come. (John 7:8)*

If we would accept Jesus' definition of success, we would discover great freedom in our ministries and strong protection from a major cause of *burnout* .

## THE DANGER OF BUSYNESS

Jesus' brothers urged Him to seize the moment. They saw a door of opportunity in Judea and pleaded with Him to run through it. On one level, Jesus had an incredible amount of work to do (to save the world)! It would seem to make sense for Him to employ every means at His disposal in order to reach as many people as possible. One might well expect to see Jesus busily rushing about, impacting as many people as possible in as short a time as possible.

Yet, in the Gospels, we do not see Jesus in crisis, overwhelmed by all that He must do. Jesus is never in a rush, fretting about being late. We don't sense an attitude of impatience when He is interrupted. Rather, He seems to genuinely enjoy people. He walked through life with an uncanny equilibrium, as though He had only one thing to do at any given time. In fact, Jesus did have only one thing to do: to fulfill His Father's will each moment. Jesus was willing to toil in Galilee as long as the Father wanted Him to. His agenda each morning was simply this: "Father, what would you have Me to do today?"

One of the strategies of our enemy is to cause us to move more quickly than we ought. Even as I write these words, I am feeling the pressure of the public arena. I have eight speaking responsibilities this coming month. Several of the messages will be new ones, needing significant development. The deadlines for my portion of this book are also next month. I don't know how I will be able to do all these things well. The temptation I face is to sacrifice the inner life in order to succeed with my outer life, to trade-off personal time with my Father in order to "pull it off." When I am under pressure, I am able to drop my head down, put my shoulder to the challenge and produce a lot in a short period of time. However, too often, it is by sacrificing intimacy and joy and a sense of walking in the Spirit.

## A SUMMARY OF THE DANGERS

We have studied the multiple dangers of public ministry, including the following:

- The danger of performance, attempting to validate ourselves by our work
- The danger of short cuts, avoiding difficulties or relying on our natural abilities instead of preparing well
- The danger of the spotlight, seeking a prominent role
- The danger of an image, crafting a public persona that does not match with reality
- The danger of success, defining our success by numbers and the weight of our reputation

- The danger of busyness, rushing through life and missing opportune times

To which of these dangers are you most vulnerable? Any one of them can drive us to *burnout*. Confess your vulnerabilities to our gracious Father right now.

In the midst of our public ministries, the Father offers three spacious places of great security. We may find protection from *burnout* in all of these things:

- The security of the Father's timing
- The security of the Father's agenda
- The security of the Father's acceptance

We will close this chapter by looking at these three places of refuge.

## THE SECURITY OF THE FATHER'S TIME

So often we *fight* time. We try to squeeze as many activities and accomplishments into any given time as is humanly possible. In some ways, we see clock time or chronological time as a commod - ity, at best, or as an enemy, at worst. Though the Scriptures do refer to this type of time, the formal passing of time, it is much more interested in another type of time: the *opportune* time. *Opportune* time is the fitting time, the appropriate time, the right time. Jesus' life seems to be dominated by this second sense of time; He lived on His Father's timetable.

Jesus walked with a sense of timing which came from His Father. We never see Him rushing about, complaining of not having enough time. There seems to be a rhythm to His life. Jesus flowed seamlessly between the public and the private realms, from the inner to the outer life.

Even in the most urgent of situations, those involving life and death, Jesus responded in a strangely unhurried manner. After He learned of Lazarus' serious illness, He remained two more days on the far side of the Jordan River before beginning to travel toward Lazarus' home. By the time He arrived, Lazarus had been dead four days (John 11:1-17). After Jairus pleaded with Jesus to come and heal his ill daughter, Jesus allowed Himself to be slowed by various "interruptions," including the woman who suffered twelve years of hemorrhaging. As with Lazarus, the daughter died even before Jesus arrived (Luke 8:41-56).

How could Jesus hold such a seemingly nonchalant attitude? He lived continually with confident trust in His Father's timing. He believed that His Father's timing was the best, even if it sometimes appeared to be bad timing. Jesus saw His timing "failures" as great opportunities for people to believe. To Jairus, Jesus said, "Don't be afraid; just believe, and she will be healed" (Luke 8:50). To His disciples Jesus said, "Lazarus is dead, and for your sake I am glad I was not there, so that you may believe" (John 11:14).

What kind of time dominates your life? Are you so committed to *clock* time that you miss out on *opportune* times? How do you evaluate the opportunities which come your way? Not only are we tempted to say "yes" to those ministries which are most public and prominent, but we are also tempted to say "yes" to those which appear most urgent. We are tempted to say "no" to those individuals whom we encounter along the way, who didn't make it onto our *Daytimers*. We are tempted to short change our personal, intimate time with our heavenly Father in the midst of the urgent press of events.

For those of us in public ministry, other people often have agendas for us. They have certain places they want us to be at certain times. We become vulnerable to *burnout* as we attempt to satisfy all of the demands upon our schedules. May God give us grace to walk in His timing, trusting Him for things undone, for things accomplished late. May we, like Jesus, always do the right things at the right time.

*Therefore Jesus told them, "The right time for me has not yet come; for you any time is right." (John 7:6)*

## THE SECURITY OF THE FATHER'S AGENDA

Jesus' brothers thought that they knew exactly what Jesus should do and when. They urged Him to "go public," begging Him to "show yourself to the world by attending the Feast of the Tabernacles in Jerusalem." They were lamenting the fact that Jesus was forgoing a larger "market" of disciples by remaining in Galilee. John then makes a startling observation. He explains their pursuit of public recognition for Jesus in this way:

*For even his own brothers did not believe in him. (John 7:5)*

How are the two things related? What does their desire for Jesus to become a public figure have to do with unbelief? John makes it sound as though you can't have it both ways: either you seek to become a public figure, or you believe God. John is drawing the contrast in the starkest of terms: who is our ultimate audience? Is it the world or is it God? Do we serve ourselves and our own agendas, or the Lord and His agenda?

After Jesus went to the Feast, He Himself drew a similar contrast:

*He who speaks on his own does so to gain honor for himself, but he who works for the honor of the one who sent him is a man of truth; there is nothing false about him. (John 7:18)*

Jesus presents two different men, both of whom are teachers. However, the similarity ends there because they are vastly different

147

from one another in terms of their motives and their agendas. One teacher is motivated by self-honor whereas the other is motivated by God's glory, seeking to magnify the honor of God. In terms of their agendas, the self-honoring one speaks his own words, whereas the God-honoring one speaks the words of God.

We feel uncomfortable with such stark contrasts as these which both John and Jesus have portrayed. We prefer more nuanced illustrations. There are no gray areas. As teachers, at any given moment in time, we are either believing God, teaching His Word faithfully, and seeking to honor Him, or else we are not. If we teach not His Word, it shows that we lack confidence (unbelief) in His Word to transform lives. If we teach in order to enhance our reputations, then we are not seeking to glorify God.

These are sobering words for men and women who teach God's Word. If we are honest, we must admit that there are times when we have been guilty of these sins that will lead us down the path of *burnout*. When we take on the burden of our own wisdom in teaching (who of us is wise enough?) or when we set out to try to project a sanitized image of ourselves (what do we gain except enslavement to the opinions of others?), we are doomed to frustra-tion. This approach to ministry is fraught with danger.

Contrast this approach to ministry with the glorious freedom that comes from teaching God's Word with confidence and with a heart solely set on the glory of God. We experience strong protection from *burnout* as we give ourselves wholeheartedly to the ministry by embracing our Father's agenda and then delighting in His acceptance of us.

## THE SECURITY OF THE FATHER'S ACCEPTANCE

We return to the beginning of Jesus' public career in the Jordan River valley where John was baptizing. Imagine the scene.

*When all the people were being baptized, Jesus was baptized too. And as he was praying, heaven was opened and the Holy Spirit descended on him in bodily form like a dove. And a voice came from heaven: "You are my Son, whom I love; with you I am well pleased." (Luke 3:21,22)*

The Father showers His favor upon His Son. What an emotional and spiritual high that must have been for our Lord! Jesus hears the most affirming words imaginable from the most important Person in His life: "You are my Son, whom I love; with you I am well pleased." Our Lord's affirmation came primarily from His heavenly Father.

Jesus understood how transitory human affirmation was, and He was unwilling to embrace the applause of the crowds. He realized that they might well find a "new and improved" hero the following week. Jesus knew that affirmation often came with "strings attached."

*But Jesus would not entrust himself to them, for he knew all men. He did not need man's testimony about man, for he knew what was in a man. (John 2:24,25)*

Each of us needs affirmation; it is a fundamental human need. This need of ours can be and is met in a variety of ways. The Father Himself has lavished His love upon us; we experience His accep-tance as we dwell in the glory of His presence. God often uses human means as well to provide ongoing approval and encourage-ment for us. Usually our spouses and our close friends provide a spacious place of love and affirmation. It is the affirmation of "the crowds," those who don't know us well, that is most fickle and least satisfying. Their perceptions are only partially informed; they don't really *know* us. When we expend our energies seeking the affirma-tion of acquaintances and church members whom we know only on a surface level, then we are in danger of *burnout*. We will be unable to satisfy all of their expectations.

It is interesting to note that Jesus is affirmed by His Father even before His ministry begins. He hasn't done anything yet (at least publicly). The Father's affirmation is not rooted in the Son's ministry but in the Son Himself. His affirmation is love-based, not performance-based. Love-based affirmation is the deepest, most satisfying of all. It doesn't contain the conditional or temporary "what have you done for me lately?" elements of performance-based affirmation.

From where do you receive most of your affirmation? Do you sense affirmation from your heavenly Father? It is critical at this point for our theology to become experiential, for our belief system to be *really* believed. Our heavenly Father treasures you, not because of what you have done nor because of what you might be able to do for Him in the future, but solely because you are you. God has made you a person of exceptional worth, precious beyond measure. Simply the fact that God has created you human imbues you with intrinsic and immense value. That good news gets even better in Christ. The Father has adopted you into His family, as His very own son or daughter. Jesus happily calls you "brother" or "sister" (cf. Hebrews 2:10-13). We are objects of His gracious love simply because in His great grace He has chosen to love us. Although we know these basic truths on a theological and intellec - tual level, may God by His Spirit drive these realities deep within the core of our souls. Then, as we remember these truths, we will be able to step into public ministry with a purity of motive, fully secure in the Father's great acceptance of us, fully protected from the terrible dangers of public ministry.

## REFLECTIONS, COMMITMENTS AND PRAYER

*Father, forgive me for those times in the ministry when I have been unduly concerned with projecting an image of myself to my people. I confess those times when I have been overly occupied with what people think about me. Protect me from the dangers of the spotlight.*

*Forgive me for being concerned more with my own agenda and less with Yours. Enable me to walk with a sense of Your timing. Give me freedom to say "no" to opportunities that are not of You and to trust You for them. Enable me to discern what You would have me to do.*

*Enable me to preach and teach with integrity, not shading hard truths to please people. Cause me to minister in full confidence that Your Word can and will transform people. Father, help me to be vulnerable and transparent with people as well as in my teaching and preaching. Cause Your glory to be my highest goal.*

*I know that everything God does will endure forever; nothing can be added to it and nothing taken from it. God does it, so men will revere him.*

*Ecclesiastes 3:14*

# 7

## *Solomon: When Life Seems Meaningless*

King Solomon was the one man in history most uniquely blessed by God with wisdom and knowledge, and yet he struggled with cynicism, emptiness and despair. As we study something of his battle, we are confronted once again with the reality that insight does not guard against *burnout*. Solomon may very well have been the most insightful man who ever lived, but toward the end, he saw his life as almost totally without meaning.

In this chapter we will discover that the true meaning of life is not wrapped up in what we do, but rather in what God is doing. We will discover that while our ministry is important, it cannot really satisfy our souls. Though God does graciously invite us to partici- pate in His work, fortunately His success is not dependent upon our performance. This perspective leads to great freedom in min- istry; our personal meaning and worth are not dependent upon a successful ministry, and we are not encumbered with the great responsibility of fulfilling an eternal work which we are simply not capable of doing. This freedom will allow us to enjoy the journey which God has prepared for us.

## An Offer You Can't Refuse

According to the Scriptures, Solomon was the only person to whom God had come with this special offer:

> *That night God appeared to Solomon and said to him, "Ask for whatever you want me to give you." (2 Chronicles 1:7)*

I shudder to think how I would have responded to that offer from God at different points of my life and ministry. How often God has protected me by not giving me what I desired! But Solomon asked God for wisdom and knowledge in order to lead His people.

> *Solomon answered God, "You have shown great kindness to David my father and have made me king in his place. Now, LORD God, let your promise to my father David be confirmed, for you have made me king over a people who are as numerous as the dust of the earth. Give me wisdom and knowledge, that I may lead this people, for who is able to govern this great people of yours?" (2 Chronicles 1:8-10)*

God was pleased with Solomon's choice and even affirmed him for not asking for a long life or riches or the death of his enemies. God promised him the wisdom and knowledge that he requested and then poured upon him an abundance of wealth, riches and honor as well.

> *"Therefore wisdom and knowledge will be given you. And I will also give you wealth, riches and honor, such as no king who was before you ever had and none after you will have."*
> *(2 Chronicles 1:12)*

There is no record in the Scriptures that God ever came to Solomon's father David with the same offer, but in Psalm 27 we seem to see David's response to the same question that God put before Solomon: "Ask for whatever you want me to give to you."

*One thing I ask of the LORD, this is what I seek: that I may dwell in the house of the LORD all the days of my life, to gaze upon the beauty of the LORD and to seek him in his temple.*
*(Psalms 27:4)*

David hungered for God. More than anything else, he desired to gaze upon His beauty and to live in his Father's house. David's consuming, passionate hunger was to seek the face of his Lord.

*Hear my voice when I call, O LORD; be merciful to me and answer me. My heart says of you, "Seek his face!" Your face, LORD, I will seek. (Psalms 27:7,8)*

Solomon asked for wisdom; David asked for God Himself. Solomon's choice was a good choice, and we must take nothing from that. God was pleased with his choice and even affirmed him, but at the same time we must say that whenever we ask for less than God Himself, we are asking for less than what God desires to give us.

We see the fruit of David's and Solomon's choices in the lives of these two men during the years that followed. David, with all of his failure and sin, grew to become a man after God's own heart. Solomon, even with all of his wisdom, became an empty, cynical and bitter man. Wisdom was not sufficient to satisfy his soul.

## DOES ANYTHING REALLY MATTER?

As we study Solomon's writing in Ecclesiastes, he hardly begins the book before the cynicism pours out of his heart.

*The words of the Teacher, son of David, king in Jerusalem:
"Meaningless! Meaningless!" says the Teacher. "Utterly meaningless! Everything is meaningless." (Ecclesiastes 1:1,2)*

"Vanity of vanities," cries the preacher. "All is vanity!" Within the
cynicism we also sense hopelessness and despair. Does anything
make a difference? Solomon then asks a key question, a question
at the very heart of his struggle.

*What does man gain from all his labor at which he toils under
the sun? Generations come and generations go, but the earth
remains forever. (Ecclesiastes 1:3,4)*

Is there anything that comes back to people as a result of the
work they do? Is there any lasting sense of completion or fulfill -
ment? The earth just seems to go on and on, generation after
generation. Nothing really seems to make any difference to Solo -
mon at all as he surveys the scene.

In his wisdom, Solomon has been watching the events around
him. He cannot find meaning in anything. There is a deep frustra -
tion in his heart as he sees great needs and yet nothing seems to
change. How often we are at that same place in our ministries. We
work hard, we seek the Lord, we serve His people faithfully by giving
all that we have, and yet nothing really seems to make a difference.
Things just keep going on the same. How do we guard against deep
frustration consuming our souls?

*I have seen all the things that are done under the sun; all of them
are meaningless, a chasing after the wind. What is twisted
cannot be straightened; what is lacking cannot be counted.
(Ecclesiastes 1:14,15)*

Solomon goes on to elaborate the various means by which he
sought to fill up his own life. As he begins his second chapter, he
describes his search for pleasure and laughter and the way in which

he cheered himself with wine and folly. He undertook great projects and built gardens and parks. He made reservoirs and water groves, bought male and female slaves, amassed silver and gold, as well as a harem. He summarizes his pursuits in this way:

> *I denied myself nothing my eyes desired; I refused my heart no pleasure. My heart took delight in all my work, and this was the reward for all my labor. (Ecclesiastes 2:10)*

Even in the midst of his great accomplishments, there remained a great sense of emptiness. Nothing had been gained by all that his hands had done.

> *Yet when I surveyed all that my hands had done and what I had toiled to achieve, everything was meaningless, a chasing after the wind; nothing was gained under the sun. (Ecclesiastes 2:11)*

Solomon was then confronted with an even greater question: with all of his great accomplishments, what would his successor do? Solomon had already done it all!

> *Then I turned my thoughts to consider wisdom, and also madness and folly. What more can the king's successor do than what has already been done? I saw that wisdom is better than folly, just as light is better than darkness. (Ecclesiastes 2:12,13)*

## SINKING INTO DESPAIR

There has never been a kingdom like Solomon's. The wisdom with which it was ruled, as well as the beauty, the wealth and the political alliances have surpassed perhaps any kingdom in history. He left nothing for his successor to accomplish; Solomon's work was complete.

Solomon knew that he would soon leave this life, for as he said, "The fate of the fool will overtake me also" (2:15). He knew that the wise man, like the fool, would not be long remembered (2:16). He came to the place where he hated life because the work he had done was grievous (2:17); he even hated all the things he had accomplished.

> *I hated all the things I had toiled for under the sun, because I must leave them to the one who comes after me. And who knows whether he will be a wise man or a fool? Yet he will have control over all the work into which I have poured my effort and skill under the sun. This too is meaningless. (Ecclesiastes 2:18,19)*

When God would take Solomon home, all the work that he had done would be left to the one who would take his place. Surely that man would not possess the wisdom with which Solomon was uniquely blessed, and the truth is, he might be a complete fool! Yet this man would have control over Solomon's great kingdom.

Solomon has been journeying on a great quest, searching for answers to profound questions which have been haunting him. He is desperately trying to find meaning for his life. What *does* the worker gain from his toil? Solomon is seeking a life of enduring, lasting value but is unable to find it in his labors. Regardless of what he accomplishes in this life, it may all disintegrate within a few months or years after he is gone.

Those of us in the ministry are tempted to find our life's meaning in our ministry because ministry has such obvious eternal aspects to it. The significance of our ministry makes it easy for us to draw our sense of personal identity and self-worth from what we do. We are tempted to focus on our competencies, on the fruit of our ministries, on the affirmation of our people, or on our reputations as spiritual leaders, and from these find our internal validation and sense of value. Yet, if we are brutally honest, as Solomon was, we must admit that the ministries we are building may not have enduring value; they may not even last until the end of the year, much less until the end of our lives.

What was the response of Solomon's heart to this under-standing? Despair!

*So my heart began to despair over all my toilsome labor under the sun. (Ecclesiastes 2:20)*

Solomon was a man of great wisdom, blessed by God with a wealth of understanding, but we have seen him spiral downward from cynicism to frustration, to emptiness, and finally to despair. How will God meet this man who is burning out on life and ministry? In chapter three of Ecclesiastes we find some of the most freeing and transforming truths about life and ministry in all of God's Word!

### NOT ENOUGH TIME

Chapter three of Ecclesiastes begins with that wonderful and familiar Scripture about time and seasons.

*There is a time for everything, and a season for every activity under heaven:... (Ecclesiastes 3:1)*

Solomon tells us that there is time for everything. This state-ment has a charming ring to it, but we really don't believe it. How often do we find ourselves saying, "I don't have enough time. I'm too busy. I don't have time to get everything done that needs to get done." Our lives and ministries seem to be characterized by a sense of rush. We are convinced that we have too much to do and not enough time.

It's not that we're wasting time. Most of the activities which demand our attention and our energy are *good* things. Just the responsibilities of the ministry and of our families are sufficient to consume all of our waking hours. When, then, do we get time to visit with our neighbors, to call old friends, to write a missionary friend, to exercise, or to read?

This Scripture tells us that we *do* have enough time to accomplish everything which God has placed before us. From where, then, does this sense of rush, of pressure, of stress come? Solomon is warning us of the dangers of doing the *right* things at the *wrong* time. When he says that there is "a time for everything," he is not merely referring to clock time (having sufficient hours in the day) but also to the *fitting* time (doing the right thing at the proper time). He says that there is a season, an appropriate time, for every activity.

We bring stress upon ourselves and heighten the likelihood of *burnout* when our *timing* is all wrong. Perhaps the most classic example for those in the ministry is working ( we say "ministering" to put a spiritual spin on it!) when we should be doing something else. We allow the ministry to supplant times when we should be playing with our children, helping with the dishes, sleeping, reading, etc.

We justify these "sacrifices" in many different ways. The needs of our people are real and urgent. Our ministries are compelling and so very important. I remember well one Thanksgiving when I was so tempted to check my e-mail for ministry-related news. It was as though my computer was demanding my attention. No! Thanksgiving is for thanksgiving and for family. The e-mail must wait until the appropriate time. We sometimes delude ourselves into thinking that our priority shifts are only short-term, yet as some of us look back, we see that our entire ministries are nothing but a continuing string of "short-term" compromises.

We have allowed our lives to go askew. We work when we should be playing. We talk when we should be listening. We sleep when we should be praying. We eat when we should be studying. We watch television when we should be communicating. Solomon says that there is time for all of these things. Our challenge is to walk in the activities God has placed before us, in His timing.

## WHAT TIME IS IT?

Solomon goes on to elaborate different seasons of life. He observes significant times of our days, weeks and years by setting before us a series of fourteen contrasts.

> *... a time to be born and a time to die, a time to plant and a time to uproot, ... (Ecclesiastes 3:2)*

As Solomon continues his list, he provides a comprehensive overview of life, covering both the most profound events of life (for example, birth and death), and also the most mundane (a time to mend and a time to throw away). Solomon is challenging us to "fit in" with the flow of life which God presents to us. He has built in certain rhythms to life, some of which are obvious, such as planting and harvesting. If a farmer tries to live counter to this rhythm, he will experience dismal failure. Solomon is challenging us to look for other, less obvious patterns of life which our Sovereign Lord brings to us, and then to fit in with those patterns.

What are your daily rhythms? When are you most alert or least communicative? What are your weekly rhythms? When are you most energized or least focused or most vulnerable to a letdown? Are there monthly or annual patterns to your life and to your ministry? I find that every two or three years I enter a restless stage in life when I want to make a major change (such as buy a different home or change to a new ministry).

We become vulnerable to *burnout* if we try to live consistently counter to the rhythms and patterns of our lives. Sometimes we must, of course, because the situation demands it: when a crisis comes, it doesn't matter if we're weary or not, we must attend to it. Other patterns of our lives are inconsistent with the leading of God for us and must therefore be resisted. For example, I know that God doesn't want me to move into a new home every two years! But much of our frustration comes as we fight against those very things which God is doing in us or bringing to us. For example, we "refuse" to be sick and keep on going as though we were well. We work when we're on vacation. We load up our schedules when our spouses or children are struggling through a time of crisis. We ignore the soft wooing of the Spirit of God to come away because of the press of events.

Solomon challenges us to recognize the seasons of our lives and to live accordingly, to do not only the right things, but to also do them at the right times. In what ways are you living and working counter to the times which God has ordained for you? We men have a wonderful gift from God to help discern this—our wives. Often they are more sensitive than we are to the seasons of life, to the need of the moment, to the appropriate time. I am slowly learning to listen to my wife when she tells me, "You've been gone too many nights this week," or "Turn off your computer; it's 5:30 and time to be with your children." Our wives can help protect us from *burnout* as we learn from them what time it is.

## Our "Job description"

After his insightful discussion of time, Solomon returns to the key question of the book and once again compels us to grapple with it.

*What does the worker gain from his toil? (Ecclesiastes 3:9)*

That question plagues Solomon's heart. Is there any sense of fulfillment or completion that comes to people as a result of the work that they do? We have each struggled with that question in relation to the work that God has entrusted to us. Does anything come back to us, filling us up in the midst of our labor?

*I have seen the burden God has laid on men. (Ecclesiastes 3:10)*

While the New International Version uses the word "burden," the New American Standard Bible uses "task...to occupy them-selves." I believe Solomon's perspective is beginning to change. Up to this point, he has been talking of the overwhelming significance of the kingdom he has built and his despair over what will happen to it when he dies. However, a "task" is not an overwhelming significant work. A task is what we give to our children to occupy them between the time they come home from school until dinner. Solomon is beginning to see that what God is doing is not depend-ent upon his great accomplishments. Rather, God assigns a task to all persons to occupy them while they are here. In His sovereignty, God then puts those tasks together into an eternally significant work.

*He has made everything beautiful in its time. He has also set eternity in the hearts of men; yet they cannot fathom what God has done from beginning to end. (Ecclesiastes 3:11)*

Many of us are task-oriented. We focus on the future, strategiz-ing and planning how to get from here to there. While this orienta-tion is good in many ways and causes us to be action-oriented and dissatisfied with the status quo, it can, on the other hand, breed a certain overconfidence in our ability to control the future. For example, we may be attracted to church growth practitioners who assure us that if we follow the system and make a certain number of neighborhood contacts and mail out so many brochures, then we will attract $X$ number of first-time visitors which eventually will result in $Y$ number of new members. Implicit in this approach is an overconfidence in our ability to direct the future and manage change. The fact is, we really cannot fathom what God is doing. We catch only glimpses here and there. It is God and God alone who controls the future.

This great truth gives us much freedom! Just as David had cried before the Lord in Psalm 31, "My times are in your hands" (v. 15), his son tells us now that God makes everything beautiful in its time. Our hearts are kept from frustration and anger when we are reminded that God has a sovereign timetable for every experience of our personal lives, our marriages, our families and our minis - tries. Even though God has blessed man with an eternal perspec - tive, we still cannot understand what He is doing! We must learn to trust in His timing and the work He is doing beyond our physical perception.

## ENJOYING THE JOURNEY

*I know that there is nothing better for men than to be happy and do good while they live. That everyone may eat and drink, and find satisfaction in all his toil—this is the gift of God. (Ecclesiastes 3:12,13)*

Future-oriented men and women often find themselves unable to enjoy the moment. We get so wrapped up in the future and in our plans that we miss out on the simple pleasures of life which are before us right now. We sometimes try to cram so much into life that we are unable to enjoy God's immediate gifts. The common experiences of life have a simple, inherent beauty in them, but it is a fragile beauty which can be too easily lost, trampled in the rush of life. At breakfast I sometimes find myself simultaneously listen - ing to the radio, reading the paper, and thinking about my plans for the day. Meanwhile, I have finished my coffee and eaten my breakfast without even being aware of it. I *love* to drink a morning cup of steaming coffee, yet somehow I miss out on the entire experience. Solomon is calling us to receive the simple pleasures of food, drink and work as gifts from God to be enjoyed in their own right and received with thanksgiving. We are being called to enjoy the journey.

Solomon almost sounds like the existentialists who say, "The past is irrelevant and the future is uncertain. We ought to enjoy our lives right now in whatever ways fill us up." However, Solomon is coming from a completely different starting point. As His view of God is becoming larger and his view of himself smaller, the pressure to produce great things is being lifted from him. Because of who God is and the way He works, His children are free to enjoy their labor and find satisfaction in what He has given to them to do.

## ONLY GOD'S WORKS ENDURE

*I know that everything God does will endure forever ...*
*(Ecclesiastes 3:14a)*

The truth is, Solomon's kingdom might not last for even one more generation. Though he has no control over what will take place after he dies, that which God does will endure forever! Solomon's focus, as well as our own, needs to be shifted from who we are and what we are doing to who God is and what He is doing. As with Solomon, our work, no matter how eloquently presented or faithfully done, may not last even to the end of the day, much less one more generation. Only what God does will remain forever.

*Everything God does will endure forever; nothing can be added to it and nothing taken from it. God does it so that men will revere him. (Ecclesiastes 3:14)*

Our hearts are set free to serve the Lord and His people with joy that overflows, rather than to be enslaved with the pressure to produce. No one can add anything to what God is doing! The most spiritual people who have ever lived—Noah, Abraham, Elijah,

David, Mary, Peter and Paul—did not add anything to God's ability to fulfill His will. God was not dependent upon Martin Luther, John Calvin, Charles Wesley, George Whitefield or the great evangelists and missionaries of our age for the building of a kingdom that will never pass away. God is sovereign over all of His work; He is in need of no one. What a joy it is to know that even though God does not need us, He desires to use us!

Just as no one can add anything to what God is doing, no one can take anything away from what He is doing either. The most evil people who have ever lived—Pharaoh, Nero, Stalin and Hitler—did not distract one iota from God's ability to fulfill His will. God is sovereign over all His works and all of His will. Just as God did not breathe a sigh of relief when Martin Luther nailed his 95 theses to the church door, He was not in fear over His ability to build His Church when Nero was taking His elect, dipping them in oil, and using them as torches to light his gardens at night. When time merges with eternity again, everything that was in God's heart to be accomplished in time will have been fulfilled. There will be no loose ends, nothing left undone. God will be the only explanation for its fulfillment, and that is why we stand in awe before Him with our hearts overflowing with worship.

> *Whatever is has already been, and what will be has been before; and God will call the past to account. (Ecclesiastes 3:15)*

## SEEKING WHAT HAS PASSED BY

Solomon is teaching us about the relationship between time and eternity. "Look around you. What do you see? It has already been there!" One day I watched a television program with my sons on the world of the microscope and the world of the telescope. We could see entire worlds in a drop of water! Through the telescope,

166

we could see the rings of Saturn. What do we do when we discover these things? Do we worship the Creator who made them? No, we worship the creature who discovers them. But what does God say? "I have been glorified for millennia by these things, and you haven't even known that they existed!"

Not only has what is already been, what will be has been before! God will call the past into account, or as the New American Standard Bible translates this, "God seeks what has passed by." Solomon is teaching us about the relationship between time and eternity. God is not looking for new things to take place in time; He is looking for old things to take place in time. Time is the realm in which God works out physically what has taken place in His heart and His mind in eternity.

We continually see this picture in the Scriptures. Jesus encouraged His disciples to pray this way.

*Your kingdom come, your will be done on earth as it is in heaven. (Matthew 6:10)*

God desires time to be a reflection of the heavenlies, or the place where those things that originate in heaven are physically expressed in the realms of this world. We see this same truth as God was instructing Moses in the building of the tabernacle.

*They [the priests] serve at a sanctuary that is a copy and shadow of what is in heaven. This is why Moses was warned when he was about to build the tabernacle: "See to it that you make everything according to the pattern shown you on the mountain." (Hebrews 8:5)*

The tabernacle that Moses built was a copy of the one in the heavenlies. We see again God's desire that time would be a reflec - tion of eternity.

The apostle John tells us this about Christ's crucifixion:

> *All inhabitants of the earth will worship the beast—all whose*
> *names have not been written in the book of life belonging to the*
> *Lamb that was slain from the creation of the world.*
> *(Revelation 13:8)*

We know that Jesus died on the cross of Calvary in the city of Jerusalem about A.D. 30. But that was when it happened in time. In the heart of God, Christ was slain before time ever began. Calvary was not an afterthought or "plan B"; the cross was God's eternal purpose fulfilled in His Son. Paul teaches us this same truth about our own salvation:

> *For he chose us in him before the creation of the world to be holy*
> *and blameless in his sight. In love he predestined us to be*
> *adopted as his sons through Jesus Christ, in accordance with his*
> *pleasure and will—to the praise of his glorious grace, which he*
> *has freely given us in the One he loves. (Ephesians 1:4-6)*

## ENTERING INTO GOD'S WORKS

Even though we are now living at the end of the 20th century, we were known by God before time began and chosen in Christ unto salvation. These same truths underlie the ministries that God has entrusted to us. He not only chose us in His Son before the creation of the world, but He prepared long in advance the works ordained for us.

> *For we are God's workmanship, created in Christ Jesus to do*
> *good works, which God prepared in advance for us to do.*
> *(Ephesians 2:10)*

Our marvelous plans, our diligent work, our innovative strate - gies, and all of our efforts which come to pass were actually conceived in eternity past. Through us, God is now bringing these works to light. He is calling the past to account and drawing it into the present, in part, through us. We are not adding to or taking away from what God has ordained from before time began. By His grace we have been given a role to play in the process, but He remains the only explanation for the fruit of our ministries.

In many ways this perspective on ministry is a humbling one. Perhaps we are not as critical to that which God is doing as we had thought. Perhaps significant church growth and the deepening maturity of our people are not the result of our excellent leadership, powerful preaching and strategic vision. Perhaps the explanation really is God, and God alone.

This humbling perspective does not, however, render our min - istries unimportant, as though we were window dressing for God. No! Rather, herein lies a glorious freedom.

## NO PRESSURE TO PRODUCE

Our Father desires to teach us, like Solomon, to see Him exalted in His sovereignty over all of His will and His works. These truths do not make our ministries irrelevant, but rather provide the only sure foundation from which we are able to work. Our hearts are set free to enjoy our labors in Him when we are reminded that we cannot add anything to or take anything away from what God is doing. He is not looking for men and women with great plans or incredible dreams to set before His people. He is not seeking those who will build great works and dedicate them to Him. God is not desirous for anyone to accomplish great things for Him that will gain the attention of those around them. Our Father is seeking those who will be vessels for His eternal works so that He alone will be the explanation for what He is doing and so that He will receive all of the glory.

Each of us has made a significant life investment in our respective ministries. Surely you desire the ministry in which you are involved to be meaningful, to have a lasting impact which will stretch all the way into eternity. These good desires and this sense of stewardship can, however, become a great, suffocating weight. Is your ownership of the ministry such that you feel responsible for its success? Do you believe that if you were removed the ministry would crumble? There is great news for you—your ministry is not really *yours*, it is God's. He ultimately is responsible for its success or failure.

In this great vision of God, the pressure for us to "produce" in ministry is removed. What God does is no longer dependent upon how well we perform. There is no lasting kingdom that we must build so that those around us will remember us or take notice of our God. We are free to walk with joy in the works that He has prepared for us, free to pursue the knowledge of God and free to be fulfilled in Him alone.

Solomon's great quest was to live a meaningful life of enduring, lasting value. He recognized that only that which God does endures forever. Yet, Solomon seemed unable to fully enter into what God was doing. As a result, frustration and despair overwhelmed him. May we learn to walk fully in our Father's works. As we do, our ministries will have lasting, eternal value and we will experience joy and freedom in the process.

## REFLECTIONS, COMMITMENTS AND PRAYER

*Father, thank You that the responsibility for a successful ministry belongs with You. I acknowledge that only that which You do lasts forever. I want to live in the glorious freedom that comes from fitting in with what You are doing. Forgive me for when I have thought too highly of myself and my ministry, thinking that it was all depend - ent upon me. Forgive me for trying to find my identity and sense of self-worth in the ministry which You have given to me. Please enable me to enjoy the journey and to receive as gifts the simple pleasures of life which You send to me. I am tired of rushing through life; help me to live with a sense of timing which comes from You. Thank You that You have made everything beautiful in its time.*

*You must speak my words to them, whether they listen or fail to listen, for they are rebellious.*

*Ezekiel 2:7*

# 8

## *Ezekiel: When Ministry Overwhelms Us*

Ezekiel taught us some of the most significant lessons in the Scriptures that protect us from losing heart in the ministry. From this great prophet we learn that God has called us to faithfulness and to trust the results to Him. We see in Ezekiel the power that flows from a vision of God's glory, a power that sets us free to minister to an "audience of One."

In 597 B.C., King Jehoiachin surrendered Jerusalem to the Babylonian army. Ezekiel, still in his twenties, was exiled to Babylon with ten thousand statesmen and soldiers. He was trained as a priest and called to the ministry of a prophet when he was thirty years old. He was one of the most passionate and dedicated prophets; he was utterly obedient to God and called to be a watchman for his people.

> *Son of man, I have made you a watchman for the house of Israel; so hear the word I speak and give them warning from me. (Ezekiel 3:17)*

Ezekiel faced incredible challenges in his ministry. At the very start, God told him that the people would not listen to him. Israel had become completely sold out to their slavery and rebellion. Their hearts were hardened before the Lord, and their stubborn-ness brought anger to God's heart, both of which resulted in their exile. But God did not forget His people. He faithfully spoke His words of redemption to them and continually called Israel to repentance. His chosen messenger was Ezekiel. But from the very beginning of his ministry, God wanted to be sure Ezekiel had no illusions about Israel's responses to the message he would bring, or to him as the messenger.

> *He then said to me: "Son of man, go now to the house of Israel and speak my words to them. You are not being sent to a people of obscure speech and difficult language, but to the house of Israel—not to many peoples of obscure speech and difficult language, whose words you cannot understand. Surely if I had sent you to them, they would have listened to you."*
> *(Ezekiel 3:4-6)*

## CALLED TO A HARDHEARTED PEOPLE

It is amazing that God contrasts His people to other nations of obscure speech and those whose different language would have made it difficult for them to understand His prophet. These were God's own chosen people! They had repeatedly experienced His deliverance, they had been the recipients of His law and had intimately known His faithfulness. Other nations, even in their difficulty of understanding, would have listened to the voice of God's prophet, but the nation upon whom God had set His affec-tions would refuse to listen.

> *But the house of Israel is not willing to listen to you because they are not willing to listen to me, for the whole house of Israel is*

*hardened and obstinate. But I will make you as unyielding and hardened as they are. I will make your forehead like the hardest stone, harder than flint. Do not be afraid of them or terrified by them, though they are a rebellious house. (Ezekiel 3:7-9)*

In the face of such a challenge in ministry and one that would take a commitment far beyond any human resource, God called Ezekiel to a level of obedience that can only be produced by His Spirit. He left no other options open to His chosen prophet. God did not allow Ezekiel to refuse His call.

*And he said to me, "Son of man, listen carefully and take to heart all the words I speak to you. Go now to your countrymen in exile and speak to them. Say to them, 'This is what the Sovereign LORD says,' whether they listen or fail to listen."*
*(Ezekiel 3:10,11)*

I am not aware of many prophets who share a level of endurance that would keep them faithful over a period of years when the people refuse to listen. Our mindset for ministry today knows hardly anything of continuing in a ministry that provides few results. However, God does not even give Ezekiel an opportunity to respond or to give any input at all about the call or the process or even to ask questions.

*Then the Spirit lifted me up, and I heard behind me a loud rumbling sound—May the glory of the LORD be praised in his dwelling place!—the sound of the wings of the living creatures brushing against each other and the sound of the wheels beside them, a loud rumbling sound. (Ezekiel 3:12,13)*

## EZEKIEL IS OVERWHELMED

The Spirit of God lifted Ezekiel up and took him away. The message heard behind him was one of glory. How can there be any glory when the people of God are enveloped by another culture, their hearts stolen away and turned against the God who had poured His love upon them to the point that they were not even willing to listen to Him?

> *The Spirit then lifted me up and took me away, and I went in bitterness and in the anger of my spirit, with the strong hand of the LORD upon me. I came to the exiles who lived at Tel Abib near the Kebar River. And there, where they were living, I sat among them for seven days—overwhelmed. (Ezekiel 3:14,15)*

There doesn't seem to be much joy in Ezekiel's call. There is no celebration in his heart over the possibility of participating in God's eternal work. He went in bitterness and anger. He was overwhelmed.

The description we find in the Word of God for the state of His people and the condition of His prophet's heart is often not far from the realities of today. Perhaps you see your people like this. Maybe your heart in the ministry is like Ezekiel's heart here. It could be that you, too, are angry and bitter in the midst of what God has chosen to do, or not to do, with you. You, too, may be overwhelmed.

How did God enable His prophet to continue in a ministry that overwhelmed him? How did our Father sustain Ezekiel's heart? There are three things that God provided for Ezekiel that enabled this man to endure: a vision of His glory, a call to faithfulness, and a commissioning to the ministry of His Word. Those are the only three things that will sustain you and me as well. Before we focus on these, let's look further into Ezekiel's ministry circumstances and the condition of His people.

## A LIVING PICTURE OF THE EXILE

Ezekiel's ministry was unique among the prophets. He taught in symbols and pictures. When God desired to teach Israel about the meaning and extent of the exile, He asked Ezekiel to model it before them in a visual allegory. Before the mes-sage was to be entrusted to Ezekiel, however, came the famil-iar warning!

> *The word of the LORD came to me: "Son of man, you are living among a rebellious people. They have eyes to see but do not see and ears to hear but do not hear, for they are a rebellious people."*
> *(Ezekiel 12:1,2)*

The rebellion of Israel caused their eyes to be blinded to God's truth and their ears to be deaf to their Father's voice. Perhaps a living illustration might get their attention and help them to under-stand the hardness of their own hearts.

> *Therefore, son of man, pack your belongings for exile and in the daytime, as they watch, set out and go from where you are to another place. Perhaps they will understand, though they are a rebellious house. During the daytime, while they watch, bring out your belongings packed for exile. Then in the evening, while they are watching, go out like those who go into exile.*
> *(Ezekiel 12:3,4)*

During the day Ezekiel packed his belongings, and at dusk he dug through the wall with his own hands. The people were watching the entire time. Then God gave wisdom to Ezekiel to apply the message to His people.

> *In the morning the word of the LORD came to me: "Son of man, did not that rebellious house of Israel ask you, 'What are you doing?'" (Ezekiel 12:8,9)*

In response to Israel's questions about Ezekiel's drama, he taught them the oracle God had prepared. This allegory was a sign of what would happen to God's children.

> *"Say to them, 'This is what the Sovereign LORD says: This oracle concerns the prince in Jerusalem and the whole house of Israel*

*who are there.' Say to them, 'I am a sign to you.' As I have done,
so it will be done to them. They will go into exile as captives."
(Ezekiel 12:10,11)*

## COSTLY MINISTRY

The price that Ezekiel paid in his obedience to God is more than
our minds can comprehend or our hearts can grasp. That our
Father would call one of His own to such a costly ministry stretches
our view of God, our understanding of His loving heart, and the
propriety of His choices. In order to teach a lesson to Israel, God
took the life of Ezekiel's wife, his joy, and did not even allow him
to mourn!

*The word of the LORD came to me: "Son of man, with one blow
I am about to take away from you the delight of your eyes. Yet
do not lament or weep or shed any tears. Groan quietly; do not
mourn for the dead. Keep your turban fastened and your sandals
on your feet; do not cover the lower part of your face or eat the
customary food of mourners." (Ezekiel 24:15-17)*

Ezekiel responded by doing as God commanded. He stated it
in such a "matter of fact" style, but we can hardly begin to imagine
the pain that filled his heart.

*So I spoke to the people in the morning, and in the evening my
wife died. The next morning I did as I had been commanded.
Then the people asked me, "Won't you tell us what these things
have to do with us?" (Ezekiel 24:18,19)*

The people seem unmoved at Ezekiel's plight and the pain that
He was bearing. They had become accustomed to his teaching in
allegories, and their question was, "What does this have to do with
us?"

*So I said to them, "The word of the LORD came to me: Say to the house of Israel, 'This is what the Sovereign LORD says: I am about to desecrate my sanctuary—the stronghold in which you take pride, the delight of your eyes, the object of your affection. The sons and daughters you left behind will fall by the sword. And you will do as I have done. You will not cover the lower part of your face or eat the customary food of mourners.*
*(Ezekiel 24:20-22)*

All of this had to do with the joy of the Father's heart and the delight of His eyes. The people that He had made His own would be taken away, and the sanctuary that He loved would be desecrated. The object of His own affections would be enslaved. His people could understand those realities only in the context of such a vivid illustration. Even in their rebellious idolatry, the temple of God was their pride and joy. That holy place would be desecrated. Their own sons and daughters would be killed by their enemies, and God would not even allow them to mourn, just as they saw in Ezekiel's drama after the death of his wife.

*You will keep your turbans on your heads and your sandals on your feet. You will not mourn or weep but will waste away because of your sins and groan among yourselves. Ezekiel will be a sign to you; you will do just as he has done. When this happens, you will know that I am the Sovereign LORD.*
*(Ezekiel 24:23,24)*

Throughout all the centuries of God's dealings with His people, there is one message that they will hear over and over again until they learn it, and that is the central message of both time and eternity. "Then you will know that I am the Lord." In whatever costly ways are necessary, to us and to God, we will learn that lesson as well.

## MY PEOPLE ARE SCATTERED

How did the people of God come to this place of hardhearted rebellion? Surely, they were responsible for their choices and actions, but much of the problem was the nature of their shep - herds. God confronted the prophets and the priests through his messenger Ezekiel; in fact, He called Ezekiel to prophesy against them.

> *The word of the LORD came to me: "Son of man, prophesy against the shepherds of Israel; prophesy and say to them: 'This is what the Sovereign LORD says: Woe to the shepherds of Israel who only take care of themselves! Should not shepherds take care of the flock?'" (Ezekiel 34:1,2)*

God had raised up the priests to look after His people and to shepherd them with His own heart. However, instead of taking care of Israel, they were more concerned with taking care of themselves.

> *You eat the curds, clothe yourselves with the wool and slaughter the choice animals, but you do not take care of the flock. You have not strengthened the weak or healed the sick or bound up the injured. You have not brought back the strays or searched for the lost. You have ruled them harshly and brutally.*
> *(Ezekiel 34:3,4)*

Rather than looking after Israel with the heart of the Father, the prophets and the priests had treated them brutally. They ruled God's house harshly, rather than responding to the hurting and the weak with the gentleness which God brings. Those who had been given the sacred trust of healing the sick and searching for the lost had become so involved in building their own lives and their own religious systems that God's children were scattered.

> *So they were scattered because there was no shepherd, and when they were scattered they became food for all the wild*

*animals. My sheep wandered over all the mountains and on every high hill. They were scattered over the whole earth, and no one searched or looked for them. (Ezekiel 34:5,6)*

God holds the shepherds accountable for the flock. As the great Shepherd, He will rescue the flock from the mouths of the shep - herds who would like to consume them. Part of God's purpose in the exile was to break down the religious system in which His people were being destroyed. He was rescuing them from a hierar- chy that was sacrificing them. God was opening their eyes to the reality of their circumstances and preparing to restore them unto Himself.

*For this is what the Sovereign LORD says: I myself will search for my sheep and look after them. As a shepherd looks after his scattered flock when he is with them, so will I look after my sheep. I will rescue them from all the places where they were scattered on a day of clouds and darkness. (Ezekiel 34:11,12)*

We have a great Shepherd who fiercely looks after His sheep. With all of His heart, God cares for the weak, the sick and the broken. He is raising up shepherds after His own heart to serve with Him and like Him in the care of His people. Sometimes we, too, become so concerned with maintaining our religious systems that our people are dying from lack of care. Pray that God would make us shepherds after His own heart.

How did God keep Ezekiel's heart in the midst of such a ministry? Ezekiel faced a hardhearted people who had con - tinually given themselves away to other gods and had adapted to a pagan system and who had been scattered because of a lack of care on the part of their shepherds. They had even been sacrificed to enhance the lives of those shepherds. Who would not burn out when called to be their prophet? Look with me at the three things in God's call to Ezekiel that protected him from losing heart in the midst of such an overwhelming ministry.

## A VISION OF GOD'S GLORY

*In the thirtieth year, in the fourth month on the fifth day, while I was among the exiles by the Kebar River, the heavens were opened and I saw visions of God. (Ezekiel 1:1)*

First of all, God began Ezekiel's ministry with a vision of Himself. As we studied earlier, vision is central for ministry if we endure to the end and are fruitful in the process. When we talk of vision, we are often consumed with the dreams of all that we would like to accomplish. Our great projects, our tremendous programs for evangelism, missions or buildings begin to fill up our eyes and our hearts. When God speaks of vision, He is calling us to a vision of Himself; the fuller our vision of God becomes, the fuller will be our lives and our ministries. All that we are and do flows out of the way in which we see God.

As Ezekiel continues with this description of God's call, he reveals the vision of the beings and the wheels. Then he relates this incredible description of God.

*Spread out above the heads of the living creatures was what looked like an expanse, sparkling like ice, and awesome. Under the expanse their wings were stretched out one toward the other, and each had two wings covering its body. When the creatures moved, I heard the sound of their wings, like the roar of rushing waters, like the voice of the Almighty, like the tumult of an army. When they stood still, they lowered their wings. (Ezekiel 1:22-24)*

The scene set before Ezekiel is "awesome." To us, something is awesome when it is incredibly great, beautiful, glorious beyond description, and breathtaking. Ezekiel was surely experiencing all of that as God was opening to him a vision of Himself and His glory.

In addition, Ezekiel is filled with a "holy terror" that begins to grip his heart, and he trembles before this awesome God who is opening Himself to be known. As the prophet hears sounds like the voice of the Almighty, he must have been overcome with fear and dread. Who trembles before the Lord anymore? Too often both pastors and people are seeking a therapeutic God, One with whom they can be "comfortable." We even want unbelievers to be "comfortable" and unthreatened as they attend our worship services, but who can be comfortable in the presence of such an awesome God?

We see this same response in Isaiah's heart as God calls him to ministry with a vision of His holiness.

> *In the year that King Uzziah died, I saw the Lord seated on a throne, high and exalted, and the train of his robe filled the temple. Above him were seraphs, each with six wings: With two wings they covered their faces, with two they covered their feet, and with two they were flying. (Isaiah 6:1,2)*

## COMFORTABLE BEFORE AN AWESOME GOD?

Seated high and exalted, God reveals Himself to Isaiah. The train of His robe is filling His temple. What an expression of the glory of His presence! The angels are gathered around His eternal throne, and even they are not "comfortable" in God's presence. They cover their faces and their feet before His holiness.

> *And they were calling to one another: "Holy, holy, holy is the LORD Almighty; the whole earth is full of his glory." At the sound of their voices the doorposts and thresholds shook and the temple was filled with smoke. (Isaiah 6:3,4)*

Isaiah must have been filled immediately with a sense of awe before a holy God who is in every way "other" than what Isaiah is. God's purity, His separation from all that is evil, and the uniqueness of His Person are revealed before Isaiah's eyes. The angels see it and cry, "Holy!" "Glory!" The earth is shaking at the sound of their voices, and the temple is filling with smoke.

> *"Woe to me!" I cried. "I am ruined! For I am a man of unclean lips, and I live among a people of unclean lips, and my eyes have seen the King, the LORD Almighty." (Isaiah 6:5)*

Not only is the earth shaking, but so is Isaiah! "I am undone!" he cries. "Woe! I am ruined! I am different from all that God is; I am sinful and I am hopeless before Him. I have seen Him, and woe is me!"

Do we see a different God than Isaiah and Ezekiel saw? Have we seen a God who reigns in holiness and glory? Does that vision cause us to tremble in His presence when we see how much less we are than He is and how depraved we are with no hope of ever being different apart from His grace and mercy? Rather than striving for people to be comfortable before Him, should we not call men and women to stand in awe and wonder as they worship before Him?

> *Then there came a voice from above the expanse over their heads as they stood with lowered wings. Above the expanse over their heads was what looked like a throne of sapphire, and high above on the throne was a figure like that of a man. (Ezekiel 1:25,26)*

## GOD'S GLORY: THE ETERNAL BATTLEGROUND

When the living creatures surrounding God's throne hear His voice, they stand with lowered wings. Then above the expanse over their heads, a throne of indescribable glory and beauty is revealed. Ezekiel could never have even begun to describe what is being set before the eyes of his heart if God had not been speaking through him. The throne "looked like sapphire," he says, and the figure seated on the throne "looked like that of a man."

*I saw that from what appeared to be his waist up he looked like glowing metal, as if full of fire, and that from there down he looked like fire; and brilliant light surrounded him. Like the appearance of a rainbow in the clouds on a rainy day, so was the radiance around him. (Ezekiel 1:27,28a)*

The prophet continues with gripping eloquence, but at the same time with a stammering description of what is beyond words and imagination. He talks of glowing metal and fullness of fire, brilliant light and the appearance of a radiant rainbow.

*This was the appearance of the likeness of the glory of the LORD. When I saw it, I fell facedown, and I heard the voice of one speaking. (Ezekiel 1:28b)*

Ezekiel is seeing nothing less than the glory of the Lord! God is beginning the ministry of His prophet with a vision of His glory. The radiance of His Person and the weightiness of His presence begin to fill Ezekiel's eyes and heart. Could anything less than a vision of the glory of God sustain his heart before such a hard-hearted, rebellious people?

God's glory is the central issue of both time and eternity. In fact, the glory of God is the great eternal battleground. It was the glory of God that Satan pursued when he fell from heaven (Ezek. 28; Isa. 14:12-15). To grasp the glory which belonged to God alone caused Satan to incite Adam and Even in the fall (Gen. 3:4,5). Satan tempted Christ to exchange the glory of God for the glory of this world (Matt. 4:8,9).

Our enemy desires to fill our eyes and our hearts with the glory of this world, which is the glory of who we are and what we are able to do. In this way he will steal from us the vision of a God whose radiance and awesome presence transcend all that we are and all that we can produce. However, the glory of our accomplishments quickly fades and pales before God whose sparkling presence and brilliant radiance totally fill the realms He has made.

In the midst of a people whose eyes could not see this God of glory and whose bankrupt religious system had become overtaken with darkness, the eternal glow of God's glory must have transformed Ezekiel. When slavery, disobedience, dead ness and depravity were all that he could see, an exalted God in His transcendent glory filled the prophet's heart with hope. Likewise, we must know in our hearts that whatever the state of God's people or the dim reality of the present circum stances, there is a throne in the heavenlies that looks like sapphire, and high above on that throne is a God who still reigns and whose glory is undiminished. This glory was the light that continually called Ezekiel onward when nothing else seemed to be working.

It is this truth that also transformed Habakkuk when all hope seemed to be lost and that which he desired from God did not seem to be happening. God reminded him of the point of His life and ministry:

> *For the earth will be filled with the knowledge of the glory of the LORD, as the waters cover the sea. (Habakkuk 2:14)*

Sometimes we, too, forget the point. When the obstacles seem overwhelming and our people do not respond and when pain and disappointment consume our hearts, we need to be reminded that God's eternal radiance is undiminished. His glory will fill the earth, and He has called us to walk with Him in that process. Just as with Ezekiel, nothing less than a vision of the glory of God will sustain us in the ministry. That glorious vision is sufficient to sustain us even in the most disappointing ministries.

## COMMISSIONED WITH GOD'S WORDS

Ezekiel had fallen face down in the midst of this glorious vision. When the brilliant light of God's radiance filled the prophet's eyes and heart, he could no longer stand in God's presence. This position not only represents the humility of Ezekiel's heart, but it pictures his dread, his awe and his worship before an exalted, sovereign and reigning God.

> *He said to me, "Son of man, stand up on your feet and I will speak to you." (Ezekiel 2:1)*

God called Ezekiel to stand, but it was only the power of God's Spirit that enabled him to do so. God raised him up and then continued to speak to him.

> *He said: "Son of man, I am sending you to the Israelites, to a rebellious nation that has rebelled against me; they and their fathers have been in revolt against me to this very day. The people to whom I am sending you are obstinate and stubborn. Say to them, 'This is what the Sovereign LORD says.'"*
> *(Ezekiel 2:3,4)*

The state of God's people, as well as their history, is set blatantly before the prophet. Not only had Israel rebelled against the Lord, but their fathers had been in revolt as well. Even though His people were stubborn and obstinate, God was faithful to speak to them. Ezekiel was now commissioned to take Israel the Word of God.

What do you say to a stubborn and obstinate people? What is the message that will transform them? Where is our hope for change? God says to Ezekiel, "Say to them, 'This is what the sovereign Lord says.'" Only the power of His Word will be sufficient to fulfill God's purposes among His people. In our next chapter we will look further into the ministry of God's Word and its transform - ing, life-giving power. We, too, have been commissioned to speak

God's Word, and any message less than that will leave His people without life and without hope.

## "PREACHING FOR RESULTS?"

God now says something to Ezekiel that is in stark contrast to our religious systems today and to the expectations of our hearts that we can hardly comprehend the meaning of the message.

> *And whether they listen or fail to listen—for they are a rebellious house—they will know that a prophet has been among them. And you, son of man, do not be afraid of them or their words. Do not be afraid, though briers and thorns are all around you and you live among scorpions. Do not be afraid of what they say or terrified by them, though they are a rebellious house. You must speak my words to them, whether they listen or fail to listen, for they are rebellious. (Ezekiel 2:5-7)*

Twice within a few minutes and in the context of a few verses, God says to Ezekiel, "You speak my Word to them whether they listen or not!" It is critical for us to understand the way in which God measures ministry. Effective ministry in the eyes of God is never measured by the response of the people. It is always meas-ured by the faithfulness of the messenger to the message that has been entrusted to him or her. We are continually measuring the effects, while God is measuring the message and the messenger. In our western culture we are pragmatists above all, and whatever "works" becomes "right." The more we adopt that mindset within the Church, the more we develop a message that can be marketed, and the more we begin to give people what they are willing to buy. However, the most important things that take place in ministry are measurable only in the heavenlies.

Of course, we pursue excellence in the ministry in every way. We pour out our hearts and our lives in service to people, and we work hard at communicating the message with relevance. Then we must trust the results to the Lord!

### "WE DID IT FOR HIM"

A few years ago, I had the privilege of teaching a seminar on "The Ministry of God's Word" at a Wycliffe Bible Translators center in South America. God gave us a wonderful time of fellowship and ministry around His Word. The brothers and sisters were very encouraging in their responses and so gracious as they shared with me the ways the Scriptures were touching their hearts. I did not understand the significance of what God was doing until our last evening. As I ate dinner with the director and his wife, she said, "I have to tell you what God has done in my heart during these days. When we came to South America many years ago, we were assigned an Indian tribe and began translating the Scriptures into their language."

You might know something of the process involved in that ministry. A linguist will go into a tribal group that does not have a written language and, after learning the spoken language, develop an alphabet and a written language. The linguist then teaches the people to read their own language. At the same time, the Scriptures are translated into the written language so this people group will be able to read the Word of God in their own heart language. This is a process that usually takes about twenty years. Though it is somewhat quicker today with the use of computers, the task is still long and tedious.

This gracious servant of the Lord continued.

*We lived at the Indian village and spent as much time with the people as we could. We were teaching the Scriptures to them as we were translating. A church was being born in their midst. As we came toward the end of the project, the people were becoming more and more involved in the production of drugs and less and less interested in the Scriptures. When we finished the translation of the New Testament in their language and scheduled the dedication service, not one person even came! I have been so angry and bitter. We gave our lives so that they could have the Word of God in their language. When we concluded what was almost a life's work, they did not even want it! I have not been able to handle the bitterness of this disappoint - ment in my heart.*

This hurting woman then said to me:

*God has been speaking to me in these days by His Word and His Spirit. He has been doing something beautiful in my heart. It is as though God has been washing His Word over my soul and healing me, and He has opened my eyes to see this all from His perspective. I am just beginning to realize now that we did it for Him! That is the only thing that makes any sense in all of this. We did it for God!*

That is the only thing that makes any sense in ministry. We do it for Him. His glory is the only motivation that can keep moving us on when the people to whom we are called do not respond. We have almost completely lost a vision for the great, eternal value of proclaiming the Person of God and the words that He speaks, just because He has called us to do it, and then trusting the results to a sovereign God who is working out His eternal purposes beyond what we can see with our eyes. We must do it for Him.

## MINISTERING TO AN AUDIENCE OF ONE

Early in his call Ezekiel learned that God is the point of ministry and that He measures the results with a completely different set of values than those which we hold. His call was to faithfulness, and so is ours.

Recently I was visiting a friend whose love, example and encouragement have been a treasured gift from the Lord. According to the way we measure ministries, he is highly successful for he pastors a very significant, growing church. As we visited, I asked how he was handling the success and affirmation he had been receiving. As we talked, I remembered well the pressures, disappointments and even depression with which he had struggled in the past. He responded this way:

> *Bill, on the continuum of "people pleasing" and "God pleasing," I have learned that the more I seek to please people, the more vulnerable I am to losing heart. The more I seek to please God alone, the freer my heart becomes. I have learned that above all, God has called me to minister to an audience of One. He alone is the highest and the only purpose for everything that I do.*

The apostle Paul said something very similar to this in his second letter to the church at Corinth. He spoke in contrast to those who would peddle the Word of God for profit.

> *Unlike so many, we do not peddle the word of God for profit. On the contrary, in Christ we speak before God with sincerity, like men sent from God. (2 Corinthians 2:17)*

Paul lays before us a powerful vision for ministry to an audience of One. Christ is the environment for all that we do, everything is done openly before the Father, our hearts are pure in their motives before the Lord, and God is the source of our lives and our ministries.

"We speak before God!" He is the point of it all, and the only purpose worthy of our hearts and our service. If we serve an audience less than Him, we will burn out along the way. God taught that truth to Ezekiel early in his ministry. He graciously brought the missionaries in South America to that understanding. My pastor friend learned it in the midst of disappointment and in the midst of success. We, too, will be sustained in the ministry when our Father's glory is our only motivation, our faithfulness the only measure along the way, and our exalted God the only point of all that we are and do.

### REFLECTIONS, COMMITMENTS AND PRAYER

*Father, thank You that You have called me to faithfulness, rather than to success. Would You give me the grace to serve You with a whole heart, and then let You measure the effectiveness of what You have called me to do? Would You fill my eyes with a vision of Your glory, and may the transcendent radiance of who You are keep moving me on when my people fail to respond? Lord, make me a shep - herd after Your own heart, and remind me that my min - istry is to an audience of One. Thank You that even in the most costly of times, You are able to sustain me.*

# SECTION 3

# The Pathway to Life: Experiencing God's Keeping Grace

*And the God of all grace, who called you to his eternal glory in Christ, after you have suffered a little while, will himself restore you and make you strong, firm and steadfast.*

*1 Peter 5:10*

*But if I say, "I will not mention him or speak any more in his name," his word is in my heart like a fire, a fire shut up in my bones. I am weary of holding it in; indeed, I cannot.*

*Jeremiah 20:9*

# 9

## *Jeremiah: Enduring Failure, Pain and Disappointment in the Ministry*

Jeremiah is often called the "weeping prophet," for he had much to weep about. In the forty years of his ministry, he never saw a single positive response to the message and the ministry God had entrusted to him. His heart was broken continually. However, as with Ezekiel, God had built into Jeremiah a steadfast heart of faithfulness that kept His prophet during these years.

Jeremiah faced not only an unresponsive, captive people, but he himself often bore the brunt of their rebellion. He faced a level of personal pain in the ministry unmatched by any other prophet except perhaps Ezekiel. Jeremiah was beaten, ridiculed, placed in stocks, thrown into cisterns and threatened with death. He cried and complained, became angry and confused and lamented that he was ever born. In spite of all this, God fulfilled His desires through Jeremiah, as He will with you and me.

What do we learn from Jeremiah that will keep us in the ministry? We learn that there is power in the words that God speaks, that His mercies which are new every morning are sufficient to enable us to endure and to fill us with hope, and that God may very well pour out our lives to fulfill His purposes.

Let's look at God's call of Jeremiah to the ministry of a prophet.

## "I Do not Know how to Speak"

*The word of the LORD came to me, saying, "Before I formed you in the womb I knew you, before you were born I set you apart; I appointed you as a prophet to the nations." (Jeremiah 1:4,5)*

Any person who would be used of God must know the roots of his or her identity, life and ministry. God wanted Jeremiah to know that the roots of his call and work went deeply into His own heart. Before he was even born, he was known of God and set apart for His purposes. He would serve with authority because the God of heaven had appointed him. Do we serve each day with that same depth of identity and authority? We can do so if we live in light of God's call and preparation of us.

*"Ah, Sovereign LORD," I said, "I do not know how to speak; I am only a child." (Jeremiah 1:6)*

How does Jeremiah respond to God's call? Just as we saw with Moses, Jeremiah is immediately caught up with his weakness and inadequacies. "You can't use me, God! I am too young. I cannot speak well!" If we are watching this scene taking place in the heavenlies, do we see God grasping His head in frustration and saying, "How could I have done it again! When am I going to learn that I need to call eloquent men and women to the ministry!" We do not see that, of course, because before God called him, He already knew that Jeremiah had nothing to say to His people that would make any difference in their lives. God was putting no confidence in the words, the eloquence, the persuasiveness, the experience or the personality of Jeremiah. All of God's confidence was in His ability to speak His words which would transform His people through this inadequate prophet whom He had chosen.

God immediately takes Jeremiah's focus off himself and his weaknesses and places it upon Him and His sufficiency.

> *But the LORD said to me, "Do not say, 'I am only a child.' You must go to everyone I send you to and say whatever I command you. Do not be afraid of them, for I am with you and will rescue you," declares the LORD. (Jeremiah 1:7,8)*

We remember well that God repeatedly told Moses all that He would do through him. God does that same thing with Jeremiah. "Who you are is not the issue, Jeremiah. Who I am is the issue. I am sending you, I am commissioning you, I am with you." To this young man who has no confidence in his own speaking ability, God says an amazing thing.

> *Then the LORD reached out his hand and touched my mouth and said to me, "Now, I have put my words in your mouth. See, today I appoint you over nations and kingdoms to uproot and tear down, to destroy and overthrow, to build and to plant."*
> *(Jeremiah 1:9,10)*

## A MINISTRY OF GOD'S WORDS

Jeremiah's ministry would be a ministry of the words of the Lord God. The One who had called him would give him the words to speak, and then bring those words to pass.

> *The word of the LORD came to me: "What do you see, Jeremiah?"*
> *"I see the branch of an almond tree," I replied. The LORD said to*

> *me, "You have seen correctly, for I am watching to see that my word is fulfilled." (Jeremiah 1:11,12)*

Using a play on words, God teaches Jeremiah about the fulfillment of His Word. In the land of Israel the almond tree was called the "watcher" since it was the first tree to bloom in the spring after the deadness and dryness of winter. Thus, God's people learned to watch for the almond tree to bloom, and then they knew that spring was upon them. In the same way, Jeremiah needed to know that God was watching over His Word and that He would bring to pass that which He had spoken. What a confidence to possess in the midst of an unresponsive people!

We do not express a great confidence today in the power of the Word of God to fulfill His purposes. The Church in North America is a great enigma to us. We hear many sermons, not only from church pulpits but from radios, televisions, and tapes. We have seminars and videos. Our presses can hardly keep up with the books we are publishing as a Church. We have more biblical insights and principles than this world could ever imagine. However, when we look for the holiness, fruitfulness and power, and the heart for missions that should flow out of all that we know and possess, they are difficult to find.

We would do well to look at places such as China, Cuba, and other countries in Asia, Latin America, and the former Eastern Block nations, where the Church of the Lord Jesus Christ is growing with incredible speed and power. While they do not have the multitude of technical tools and church growth principles that we possess, there is generally a sincere desire to teach the Scriptures faithfully. God builds His Church on the ministry of His words.

Much of what is being given as ministry today in the Church in North America is actually a presentation of our own words. We have so much to say today in God's Church! We do not find many like Moses and Jeremiah who shrink back in the face of speaking before God's people. We have fallen in love with our own eloquence and ideas, our insights and principles, our stories and homilies. It is not at all unusual for a pastor to stand in the pulpit and use a Bible verse as a basis for twenty minutes of his own thoughts. This is a recipe for *burnout.*

Perhaps we are not aware of the pride involved in such a self-promoting experience. God never permitted the prophets to give their own words, ideas, impressions or solutions to His people, nor did He permit the disciples or the apostles to do so. Even Jesus said, "The words I say to you are not just my own. Rather, it is the Father, living in me, who is doing His work" (John 14:10). We are greatly in need of a revival of the ministry of God's Word in His Church today!

Jeremiah was confronted with a religious system which was built on the words of men rather than the authority of God's Word. God sets this harsh and frightening judgment upon His people who pursue only what they want to hear rather than the truths which come from their Father's heart. We would do well to listen to this warning also.

*A horrible and shocking thing has happened in the land: The prophets prophesy lies, the priests rule by their own authority, and my people love it this way. But what will you do in the end? (Jeremiah 5:30,31)*

## A REVIVAL OF WORSHIP; A FAMINE FOR PREACHING

As I was preparing for this writing, I sought the counsel of a pastor who shares a passion for worship and for the preaching of the Scriptures. While we talked, I asked "How can we be in the midst of a revival of worship and in the midst of a famine for the hearing of the Word of God at the same time?" His answer astounded me!

*Our worship music is so powerful both in its lyrics and its melodies. As our people are worshiping, their hearts are carried passionately Godward. Then the pastor gets up to preach. He feels he must sustain the passion and the power the people have experienced in worship, but he does not have confidence in the preaching of the Scriptures to do that. So instead, he places his confidence in gripping illustrations, emotional stories, and insightful examples.*

Look at the way in which God describes the power of His Word through the prophet Isaiah:

*As the rain and the snow come down from heaven, and do not return to it without watering the earth and making it bud and flourish, so that it yields seed for the sower and bread for the eater, so is my word that goes out from my mouth: It will not return to me empty, but will accomplish what I desire and achieve the purpose for which I sent it. (Isaiah 55:10,11)*

The rain and snow are pictures for us of God's creative, life-giving Word. As the rain and snow stimulate the earth to fruitfulness, causing it to bring forth seed for the sower and bread for the eater, the words that God speaks bring life to those for whom He has given ears to hear. God is able to create life when there is no life by means of His Word and His Spirit!

I was invited to speak for the annual staff conference of an overseas mission base. One afternoon I spoke on the depth of God's forgiveness, flowing out of the blood of His Son shed for us on Calvary. We looked at God's glorious Word and saw how He takes away our sin as far as the east is from the west (Ps. 103:12). He blots out our transgressions and remembers our sins no more (Isa. 43:25). In God's forgiveness, He has disarmed the powers of darkness concerning anything they might use against us (Col. 3:13-15) and cleansed our consciences from the past (Heb.

9:11-14). We were gripped by the truth that godly sorrow brings a repentance without regret (2 Cor. 7:10).

Surely, the depth of God's forgiveness in His Son, the fullness of His mercy and grace overwhelm our hearts, and we want to cry out, "That is absolutely too good to be true!" That was exactly the case for a young woman in attendance.

That evening her husband asked if we could visit together. As we talked, his wife poured out an incredible load of guilt, condemnation and fear. Before she had come to know the Lord, she had been a promiscuous young woman. She knew the Scriptures well that I had taught, but the enemy had powerfully enslaved her to her past so that the guilt and regrets of it all had stolen away any freedom. Satan had convinced her that she could never be what her husband deserved, never have children, and never be fully used in ministry because of her past. The fear, regrets, guilt and shame of her sin were always before her. She knew nothing of a cleansed conscience or a heart free from regrets.

We talked, we studied further, and we prayed, but she had been beaten down for so long by Satan that it all seemed too good to be true. Though I left for a week of ministry with another group of missionaries, I saw her and her husband again before I returned home. With joy and thanksgiving she told me of the freedom God had brought to her through His Word. The great battle was over. God "had sent forth His Word and healed her" (Ps. 107:20).

What words could I have brought from my own mind to that hurting woman that would have accomplished this great work in her heart? What stories or principles could I have thought of that would have set her free and healed her? I do not have the power to do that because my words do not create life in people!

## COMPARING OURSELVES WITH OURSELVES

When God gives us a vision for the ministry of His Word, we often face new battles in our congregations. Sometimes the local pastor is compared to great radio and television preachers. I was visiting with the faithful pastor of a very ordinary church in an average size town in the U.S. We were talking together about the power of God's Word in ministry and the great need today for biblical preaching, just as we have seen in God's call to Jeremiah. During the discussion he said that recently a man in his congregation had come to him and said, "Why should I come to hear you when I can listen to even better preachers on the radio?" Of course, this pastor's heart was crushed!

The comparison that is taking place in God's Church today, as we put the great writers, pastors, evangelists and preachers on display before our people, is a deadly game. They look at these beautiful, eloquent, successful religious entrepreneurs and say, "Why isn't my pastor like that? Why isn't our church like that?" Who measures up to the ideals of beauty and success that the Church loves to elevate in our hunger for significance?

I love the great preachers, and I thank God for them. However, when this man who loves the preaching on television better than his own pastor's has a child who becomes critically ill in the middle of the night, who will he call? Will those preachers be there to hold his hand, to offer comfort and to pray with him?

When was the last time you went to a pastors' conference in which the main speaker was one who had pastored the same church for twenty-five years. As he was introduced, the host said, "No one has ever heard of this man. But he has pastored the same church of eighty people for many years.

He has taught the Scriptures faithfully and shepherded his flock with the heart of God. He is a man of integrity and vision. We want to learn from him how God can give us a ministry like that."

That has probably never happened and perhaps it never will because we keep measuring the wrong things. The truth is, that pastor is on the front line of the battle, and pastors like him are the real heroes in the Church. Our expectations have been warped by the celebrity religious culture in which we find ourselves today.

There is no more demanding job nor a more pressure-filled ministry than pastoring a local church. To bring a fresh message from the Scriptures each week, to meet counseling needs, to lead with vision, and to meet the expectations of the people is more than anyone can handle. Then when we are continually compared with the "super-stars of the gospel," we tend to lose heart!

## LIKE A FIRE IN OUR BONES!

Jeremiah delighted in the Word of God for the sake of his own soul as well as for the ministry set before him.

> *When your words came, I ate them; they were my joy and my heart's delight, for I bear your name, O LORD God Almighty. (Jeremiah 15:16)*

Ezekiel, like Jeremiah, shared a similar experience. After the vision of God's glory and the call to faithfulness, God set an amazing experience before him.

> *"But you, son of man, listen to what I say to you. Do not rebel like that rebellious house; open your mouth and eat what I give you." Then I looked, and I saw a hand stretched out to me. In it was a scroll,... (Ezekiel 2:8,9)*

When Ezekiel looked at the scroll, it was filled with hard and bitter words. Mourning, lamentation and woe were written on both sides.

*And he said to me, "Son of man, eat what is before you, eat this scroll; then go and speak to the house of Israel." So I opened my mouth, and he gave me the scroll to eat. (Ezekiel 3:1,2)*

"Eat the scroll, Ezekiel! Then go and speak to my house." How could Ezekiel feed on something so distasteful as what he had read? But in obedience to the Lord's command, he ate.

*Then he said to me, "Son of man, eat this scroll I am giving you and fill your stomach with it." So I ate it, and it tasted as sweet as honey in my mouth. He then said to me: "Son of man, go now to the house of Israel and speak my words to them."*
*(Ezekiel 3:3,4)*

When Ezekiel ate the scroll, it was as "sweet as honey." Then God said, "Now go speak my words to my people." However, before Ezekiel could speak God's Word with power and authority in a way that brought the life of God to His people, that Word first had to come alive within him. That happened in the process of his own obedience as he fed on the Scriptures.

The Word of God brings life to the preacher as well as to the people. How many men and women, after years of telling stories and sharing their own words and thoughts, lose heart because they see no changes in people? Like Ezekiel and Jeremiah, God has called us to love His Word, to feed upon, study and obey it, and to teach the Scriptures. Do not teach about the Scriptures. Do not use the Scriptures in your teaching. Do not teach principles from the Scriptures. Teach the Scriptures! Ask God to build into your heart a passion for His Word. Then bring the Scriptures to your people with that same passion and ask God to move their hearts to "sing in worship" with you as you exalt God in His life-giving Word!

When we minister in this way, we have the great joy of seeing God transform people before our very eyes by the power of His Word. If we do not see it now, we will live with the confidence that God will fulfill His Word in His time. That hope and that joy will keep us in the ministry.

It was that hope which kept Jeremiah in the ministry even in the most devastating afflictions and painful disappointments. When his faithfulness to God's call and His prophetic proclamation of His message resulted in rejection and persecution, he cried out to God with strong complaints, confusion and deep despair. His words follow:

*Whenever I speak, I cry out proclaiming violence and destruction. So the word of the LORD has brought me insult and reproach all day long. (Jeremiah 20:8)*

How could he continue to speak God's Word at such a cost? However, how could he keep from speaking forth the message God had entrusted to Him?

*But if I say, "I will not mention him or speak any more in his name," his word is in my heart like a fire, a fire shut up in my bones. I am weary of holding it in; indeed, I cannot.*
*(Jeremiah 20:9)*

May God's Word become the fire in our bones! May we, by God's grace, be faithful like Jeremiah to speak forth the message God has entrusted to us even in the midst of the disappointments and the pain of serving Him and even when people do not respond as we had hoped.

### BECAUSE OF GOD'S MERCIES, WE ARE NOT CONSUMED

Jeremiah was devastatingly honest with God and with His readers concerning his afflictions and pain in the ministry. He knew that God was ultimately behind all that was happening to him, and to some degree that understanding brought even greater despair and confusion.

> *Who can speak and have it happen if the Lord has not decreed it? Is it not from the mouth of the Most High that both calamities and good things come? (Lamentations 3:37,38)*

Like the prophet of old, the knowledge that all of our times and experiences, each of our afflictions and disappointments are ordained by a sovereign God brings at once a deep sense of security and at the same time some confusion and frustration. Look at how Jeremiah describes what is taking place in his circumstances and in his heart.

> *I am the man who has seen affliction by the rod of his wrath. He has driven me away and made me walk in darkness rather than light; indeed, he has turned his hand against me again and again, all day long. (Lamentations 3:1-3)*

Jeremiah is having a hard time understanding how the God who has called him can be the One who is ordaining such affliction in his life. He goes on to talk of how God has besieged and surrounded him with bitterness and hardship (vs. 5), how He has walled him in and weighed him down with chains (vs. 7). Have you ever felt like that in the ministry? I have! The prophet speaks of God's shutting out his prayers (vs. 8) and barring his way (vs. 9), of leaving him without help (vs. 11) and making him His target (vs. 12). Jeremiah says that God pierced his heart (vs. 13), filled him with bitter herbs (vs. 15) and trampled him in the dust (vs. 16). How does he summarize his feelings?

*So I say, "My splendor is gone and all that I had hoped from the LORD." (Lamentations 3:18)*

How can anyone continue to serve the Lord in the midst of such affliction and in the face of such pain and disappointment? Is it possible for God to sustain the hearts of His servants when all that they had hoped of Him is gone? Even when Jeremiah says, "My soul is downcast within me" (vs. 20), God is there!

*Yet this I call to mind and therefore I have hope: Because of the Lord's great love we are not consumed, for his compassions never fail. They are new every morning; great is your faithfulness. I say to myself, "The LORD is my portion; therefore I will wait for him." The LORD is good to those whose hope is in him, to the one who seeks him;... (Lamentations 3:21-25)*

There is hope for Jeremiah because God's mercies are new every morning, and great is His faithfulness! In the midst of all this devastation around and within him, God gives Jeremiah the light to say in the darkness, "God is my portion! I will wait for Him! I have hope!"

Just as Paul said to the church at Corinth, "Therefore, since through God's mercy we have this ministry, we do not lose heart" (2 Cor. 4:1), it was the Father's mercy that sustained Jeremiah long ago and filled his heart with hope. God had not left him, even though through His sovereign hands were poured more pain and disappointment than the prophet thought he could bear. God's glorious presence was there and was sufficient to keep Jeremiah's heart.

What did God's "glorious presence" look like for Jeremiah? How did God's mercies touch his life in the midst of these great trials? Surely these were "severe mercies" that God brought to His prophet. Jeremiah was met by God and sustained. His pain was not diminished, nor were his circumstances changed, but he knew he was not alone; he had not been abandoned by his Father. God was there and would carry him through.

No matter what pain, affliction and disappointment we are facing right now, God will meet us there and enable us to hope in Him. Even if the afflictions are about to overwhelm us, God is able to surround us with His mercies in our present circumstances and keep our hearts. Our Father is able to give us all that we need to endure.

## ENDURANCE: A SIGN OF GOD'S CALL

Endurance may very well be the most important character quality in ministry. The ability to keep going when we are facing overwhelming obstacles and incredible hurts and pressures is one of the most visible marks of a man or woman who is called of God. As Jesus was sending His disciples out into ministry, He said this:

*All men will hate you because of me, but he who stands firm to the end will be saved. (Matthew 10:22)*

We often refer to Hebrews chapter eleven as "faith's hall of fame," but faith is only the major theme when we lift that chapter out of its context and isolate its message. When we broaden the context from chapters ten through twelve, the major theme that emerges is no longer faith but endurance. This is what the writer says as he comes to the close of his tenth chapter:

*You need to persevere so that when you have done the will of God, you will receive what he has promised. (Hebrews 10:36)*

Hebrews chapter eleven, then, is filled with examples of those who through the faith God entrusted to them were able to endure. Abraham endured in the midst of this world because God revealed to him another kingdom that possessed a greater depth of reality. Moses chose to endure ill treatment with the people of

God rather than to enjoy the passing pleasures of sin. We have one example after another of men and women of God who persevered by means of their faith.

> *Therefore, since we are surrounded by such a great cloud of witnesses, let us throw off everything that hinders and the sin that so easily entangles, and let us run with perseverance the race marked out for us. (Hebrews 12:1)*

With all these models of the faith surrounding us, we are also called to persevere in the race which God has marked out for us. Whatever the obstacles, disappointments, persecutions and failures, God asks us to hold on to Him and to continue to walk in all that He has set before us. The writer now reminds us of the supreme example of endurance.

> *Let us fix our eyes on Jesus, the author and perfecter of our faith, who for the joy set before him endured the cross, scorning its shame, and sat down at the right hand of the throne of God. Consider him who endured such opposition from sinful men, so that you will not grow weary and lose heart. (Hebrews 12:2,3)*

When the Lord Jesus fills our vision, we are transformed into His likeness by the power of the Holy Spirit, and His model moves us to endurance. When we feel that no one else has ever experienced the depth of pain, loneliness or affliction that we are experiencing now, we must remember Jesus!

> *In your struggle against sin, you have not yet resisted to the point of shedding your blood. And you have forgotten that word of encouragement that addresses you as sons: "My son, do not make light of the Lord's discipline, and do not lose heart when he rebukes you, because the Lord disciplines those he loves, and he punishes everyone he accepts as a son." (Hebrews 12:4-6)*

The writer reminds us here that we have not resisted in our battle against sin to the degree that Jesus struggled. We can visualize His battle in the garden which was so intense that the blood was pouring out of Him as sweat. Then we see the stripes from the beatings, the spears and the nail prints. We have not come to that place yet. I will never forget the day I looked at that Scripture and responded, "That is the greatest understatement I have ever read in my life! I haven't even come close to that depth of costly obedience!"

*Endure hardship as discipline; God is treating you as sons. For what son is not disciplined by his father? (Hebrews 12:7)*

The writer now tells us of God's ministry of discipline in our lives that builds into us the strength and power needed to endure all the way to the end of the race that our Father has set before us—the race that will end before His glorious throne when we see His face and hear Him say, "Well done!"

## GOD PROMISES THE CROSS

We have talked about our struggles with expectations in the ministry. Often the expectations of others bring us so much pressure that we lose heart and sometimes our expectations of ourselves are so unrealistic that we essentially give up. However, there is another set of expectations that gets us into even deeper trouble, and that is our expectations of God and what He will do with us and for us. We do not want to hear about God's disciplines and the warning to not lose heart in the process. His disciplines are painful and costly. Many of us are not willing to pay the price of the process in which God conforms us to the image of His Son, building His heart into us, and preparing us for a ministry of fruitfulness.

So many of us go into a pastoral or missions ministry with expectations that are way out of proportion to either God's call or to His promises. Sometimes we assume that people will love and respect us and respond to our message, and that we will have great success. If this is the case with you, you have not heard God clearly. He did not promise you affirmation and success; He promised you the cross.

How many times have we read the apostle Peter's introduction to his first letter? Let's look at that again. Peter is writing to those who, because of the great persecutions in the first century Church, had been scattered. Many had lost their businesses, their homes, and even family members in the very costly spread of the gospel. Peter is writing to lift their eyes to see God in the midst of their circumstances. He desires to encourage their hearts and to give them hope.

> *Praise be to the God and Father of our Lord Jesus Christ! In his great mercy he has given us new birth into a living hope through the resurrection of Jesus Christ from the dead, and into an inheritance that can never perish, spoil or fade—kept in heaven for you, who through faith are shielded by God's power until the coming of the salvation that is ready to be revealed in the last time. In this you greatly rejoice, though now for a little while you may have had to suffer grief in all kinds of trials. (1 Peter 1:3-6)*

Even in their overwhelming pain, pressure and loss, Peter says, "You need to remember that you have a hope that is alive. Your hope is not limited to this physical, temporal realm, but you have an inheritance that is imperishable and waiting for you in heaven. You have a life that is protected by the very power of God, even though for a little while you have experienced much grief in the midst of these afflictions."

I would love to have been there when this letter was first read among the churches! I can see the people immediately standing and crying out in one voice, "Say what, Peter? Would you run that by me one more time? A hope that is alive, an inheritance imperishable, and a life protected by the power of God? What are you talking about? Where was

God when they confiscated my business, Peter? Where was God when they burned down my house? Where was God when they took my children away from me? Where was God when they raped my wife? Peter, where was God's protection when they led my husband to the arena?"

This is Peter's answer: "Where was God? He was on His throne, ruling in the affairs of men and women, and caring for His people. And even in this, not for one moment, not in any relationship or experience, not in any circumstance, were you outside of the protection of His power!"

You see, the Word of God is written for real people, in real life relationships, in real life ministry situations. It is not given to people in make-believe relationships and circumstances. We get into trouble in ministry when we expect anything more than the cross and the call to lay down our lives for Christ and His kingdom.

## COULD I SPEAK WITH YOU ABOUT YOUR JUSTICE?

Jeremiah got into trouble in this area of expectations. When God did not function the way Jeremiah anticipated he would, the prophet demanded an explanation.

> *You are always righteous, O LORD, when I bring a case before you. Yet I would speak with you about your justice: Why does the way of the wicked prosper? Why do all the faithless live at ease? (Jeremiah 12:1)*

Jeremiah had no difficulty understanding God's righteousness. He served a holy God, a righteous judge. But God's justice needed an explanation! The wicked prospered, and those who had no faith lived at ease. Sometimes we, too, live with the subtle expectations that since we are serving God with a whole heart, there should be an extra measure of protection and provision for us in the process. We look at people who seem to curse God with every other breath, and they have great success in their business, they have beautiful families, and they are happy, healthy and wealthy. Then we look at the way we and other brothers and sisters desire only to serve the Lord and are willing to sacrifice to do so, but rather than honor, we experience sickness, poverty, pain, aloneness and lack of respect. Sometimes we, like Jeremiah, would like to cry out to God, "Can you explain your justice to me? This isn't fair!"

Look at God's response to Jeremiah.

*If you have raced with men on foot and they have worn you out, how can you compete with horses? If you stumble in safe country, how will you manage in the thickets by the Jordan? (Jeremiah 12:5)*

"Jeremiah, if you cannot handle the normal day-to-day disappointments and confusion, how will you handle it when things really get difficult? If you cannot keep up with men, how will you run with the horses? What will you do when the circumstances far exceed your strength, your understanding and your resources? Toughen up, Jeremiah! Stop whining! If you are having difficulty now, what will you do in the coming captivity?" Sometimes God tells us to toughen up, stop whining, hang in there and persevere in the ministry, even when we don't understand or when disappointments overwhelm us.

## GOD'S GREAT INEFFICIENCY

When we are confronted with our expectations of God in the ministry and His call to persevere, we need to know that one of the reasons we must endure is because God is greatly inefficient in His Person, His ways and His works. Somehow we have come to believe that heaven functions like a "great, eternal IBM corporation," but it is not so. Nothing about God is ever "measured out"; everything about Him and His work is "poured out." God *lavished*

His love upon us in His Son. His pardon is *abundant.* and His grace *overwhelms* our sin. It will also be so with you and me. Frankly, one of the reasons we must endure is that God keeps pouring out the lives of His people to fulfill His purposes.

We receive in our church bulletin each month a flyer published by Tyndale House Publishers entitled, "The Church Around the World." In August of 1996 I read this report on Sudan.

### Millions of Christians Killed in Sudan

*During the past three decades, about 3 million people have been killed in the Sudan because of their religious beliefs, and the nation's Christians, who make up 20 percent of the population, are most at risk. In 1992 the military junta in Khartoum declared a "holy war" against non-Muslims. According to witnesses, entire Christian villages have been annihilated and congregations have been burned to death in their churches. More than 10,000 women and children have been kidnapped and sold as slaves.*

Though perhaps on a lesser scale, this is happening in many countries around the world. In fact, there have been more Christian martyrs in the 20th century than in all of the other centuries combined. God pours out His people to fulfill His purposes, and we must expect nothing less.

I first began to think of this concept when we sent out a young man from our church to work among the Indians of Montana. Jim preached during our morning worship before he was commissioned and sent out to this new ministry. A few days later at our pastoral staff meeting one of the pastors said, "Someone made an interesting comment to me. He said, 'It is too bad that Jim is going to work among the Indians. He really is a good preacher!'" Of course, Jim is not the first good man that God has "wasted" on the Indians. Jonathan Edwards, perhaps the greatest intellect and theologian to ever set foot on American soil, ended his ministry among the Indians of New England.

## WHY THIS WASTE?

Thinking of being "wasted" reminds me of the way Mary anointed Jesus with the vial of expensive perfume before He went to the cross. Our Lord had dinner with Lazarus, whom Jesus had raised from the dead, and his sisters Mary and Martha.

> *Then Mary took about a pint of pure nard, an expensive perfume; she poured it on Jesus' feet and wiped his feet with her hair. And the house was filled with the fragrance of the perfume.*
> *(John 12:3)*

As Judas was watching this take place, he was aghast! This perfume was worth an entire year's wages. Just think of what could be done with that much money!

> *But one of his disciples, Judas Iscariot, who was later to betray him, objected, "Why wasn't this perfume sold and the money given to the poor? It was worth a year's wages." He did not say this because he cared about the poor but because he was a thief; as keeper of the money bag, he used to help himself to what was put into it. (John 12:4-6)*

As Matthew describes this same incident, it is not only Judas who responds this way, but all of the disciples cry out, "Why this waste!" (Matt. 26:8). Jesus revealed that it was completely proper that this valuable perfume should be poured out on Him.

> *"Leave her alone," Jesus replied. "It was intended that she should save this perfume for the day of my burial. You will always have the poor among you, but you will not always have me."*
> *(John 12:7,8)*

Of course, in this incident Mary is anointing Jesus before His death and burial and is a picture of something else very costly about to be poured out: the precious life and blood of the spotless Lamb of God. When we take away all of the illusions with which we live concerning ourselves and realize that we were dead in our sins when God gave His Son for us, that we were God's enemies when Christ died for us, we, too, might cry out in light of it all, "Why this waste? Why was God's only Son given for me?" It is God's nature to be "wasteful."

When we speak of God's great inefficiency in ministry, we are, of course, talking about human measurements of the way in which things are done, a concept to which God is not confined. Efficiency is very important to us because of our limited resources. However, God never needs to consider efficiency because His resources are limitless. The truth is, whatever our definition of "efficiency" is, God is not it!

Some years ago, I had the opportunity to take my son Joel with me to Ecuador, where I taught seminars in Quito and Shell Mera for missionaries. Shell Mera is the town from which Jim Elliot, Nate Saint, Roger Youderian, Ed McCully and Pete Fleming went out when they searched for the Auca Indians. While we were there, Joel and I had the privilege of flying out to the Auca village Toñapare. Dayuma, the first Auca convert, was there and took Joel on a personal tour of the village. It was one of the most moving experiences of his life.

I had previously traveled to Toñapare with some missionary friends a few years earlier. On that trip, we crossed the Curaray River, walked on Palm Beach where the five men were slain, and stood around the common grave where they were buried. The school teacher in the village had gone with us to the other side of the river. He was not an Auca and had come to the village after the murders. He had been personally discipled by Nate Saint, the jungle pilot with Missionary Aviation Fellowship. As we stood around the grave, he told us the story from the perspective of the

Indians: how the missionaries had guns and chose not to shoot the Indians, and after the murders, they heard the sound of singing in the trees.

This school teacher continued, "The last thing Nate Saint told me was, 'Don't ever give up. Whatever happens in your life, don't give up on God. Keep trusting Him.'" That was the legacy which Nate Saint had left this young man.

### IT DOESN'T MAKE SENSE!

In preparation for that trip, I had asked Joel to read Elisabeth Elliot's book *Through Gates of Splendor* which tells the story of the five missionaries and their outreach to the Aucas. The book I purchased was the twenty-fifth anniversary edition of this incident. In the introduction, the author made some interesting comments.

> *There is always the urge to oversimplify, to weigh in at once with interpretations that cannot possibly cover all the data or stand up to close inspection. We know, for example, that time and again in the history of the Christian Church, the blood of martyrs has been its seed. So we are tempted to assume a simple equation here. Five men died. This will mean X-number of Auca Christians. Perhaps so. Perhaps not. Cause and effect are in God's hands. Is it not the part of faith simply to let them rest there? God is God. I dethrone Him in my heart if I demand that He act in ways that satisfy my idea of justice. It is the same spirit that taunted, "If Thou be the Son of God, come down from the Cross." There is unbelief, there is even rebellion, in the attitude which says, "God has no right to do this to five men unless...."*[1]

1  Elisabeth Elliot, *Through Gates of Splendor*, Tyndale House Publishers, 1981, p. 269.

The truth is, it is difficult to know how strong the church is among the Aucas. But by almost any measure, it does not make much sense to us that God would pour out the lives of five godly young men without more obvious fruit in that place. God is greatly inefficient in His Person, His ways, and with His people.

I must tell you that when I teach this concept in the Church in North America, people have great difficulty understanding it. We worship efficiency. To link God with something so negative as "inefficiency" seems almost blasphemous. However, when I teach this on the mission field, the brothers and sisters there have no difficulty understanding it at all, because they live with it every day.

Not too long ago, I had the privilege of teaching these truths on another mission base. After that session I was having dinner with some of the missionaries. During our fellowship, one of the missionaries said, "Bill, while you were teaching, I was picturing a mountainside filled with beautiful wild flowers. God does not make just a few flowers; He makes millions and pours them out along the side of the mountain." Then another missionary said, "Most of those flowers will never even be seen by people. God just pours them out for His own pleasure!"

Another missionary then commented, "You know what I was thinking? I was thinking of great needs on the field here. We pray and pray that God will raise up laborers for the harvest. It doesn't make sense to us that with all of the opportunities we have for ministry, God does not provide more workers. Then we hear that someone has been called and appointed to the field! It will take almost three years for them to raise their support. Finally, they arrive and we are shouting, 'Praise God!' Then almost beyond belief, their support does not hold or there is sickness in the family or relationship problems arise on the base, and they return home. It doesn't make any sense! All of that time, all of those prayers, all of that money, and they do not even finish their first term!" God is greatly inefficient!

## OUR MINISTRY BEFORE THE ANGELS

There is another reason for Jeremiah's need to "run with the horses" and our need to endure in God's call upon our lives, and that reason is our ministry before the angels. We often become convinced that we are the center of God's purposes. We are the glory and the crown of His creation, but perhaps He has raised us up to reveal Himself to the angels. Paul said to the church at Corinth, "We are a spectacle to the angels" (1 Cor. 4:9). To the church at Ephesus, he said the following:

> *His intent was that now, through the church, the manifold wisdom of God should be made known to the rulers and authorities in the heavenly realms, according to his eternal purpose which he accomplished in Christ Jesus our Lord. (Ephesians 3:10,11)*

There is a story in the Scriptures that ties together these two concepts of God's great inefficiency and our ministry before the angels. It is, of course, the story of Job. The book begins with the angels of God gathering in His presence, and Satan is among them. It is not the enemy who brings up the subject of Job; it is God. "Have you considered my servant Job?" the Lord God asks the Evil One. Satan responds.

> *"Does Job fear God for nothing?" Satan replied. "Have you not put a hedge around him and his household and everything he has? You have blessed the work of his hands, so that his flocks and herds are spread throughout the land. But stretch out your hand and strike everything he has, and he will surely curse you to your face." (Job 1:9-11)*

God gave Satan permission to work in Job's life for he could not have touched Job's life apart from God's permission, for He is sovereign even over evil. A great battle began to unfold. Job lost his health, his wealth, his family and his bearings. His friends brought the circular, endless, mindless reasoning of the world which frustrated his heart and increased his pain. Elihu, however, brought God's perspective. God then drew word pictures in Job's mind so that he could visualize God's power and His sovereignty over all of creation and all of His will. Job was transformed in that great vision of God. He repented, prayed for his friends, and God restored him.

We find one of the most beautiful pictures in all of God's Word at the end of the book of Job. When God restored him, He gave Job twice as much as he had before in riches, flocks and herds, but only the same number of children. That was so because he had, in fact, not lost the first ones who had died in Satan's attack. They were waiting for him in heaven when he got there!

Do you realize that God never told Job the point of the book? Job never knew that he had become a battle point in eternity, and that God was pouring out his life in order to vindicate Himself before the angels! The book is filled with Job's questions. Why is this happening to me? If only there was an umpire who could mediate between us! (Job 9:32,33). Why have you made me your target? (Job 7:20) God never gave Job the answers he was seeking, but He did give Job Himself in the battle. God did not owe Job an explanation for his experiences. God poured out the life of this man, and Job never knew why.

## WE MAY BE POURED OUT

Although we are here to be used of God, what God does with us might not be what we hope for or what we expect Him to do. What God does with us might never be measurable. He may choose to pour out our lives in a way that we never anticipated, or for what seems small to human eyes. We must leave room for the sovereignty of God! Yet, as we learn from Jeremiah, we can be poured out without being burned out, because God is there.

The next time we are tempted to yield to sin, to give up on a marriage, or to bail out of a ministry, it might be a good idea to ask the following: "Have I become a battle point in eternity? Has the enemy issued a challenge to the Lord God before the angels and said, 'He will never keep walking with you through this!'?" God has said, "You watch. You watch!" It may very well be that God will reveal His glorious purposes to the angels through us as we hold onto God and continue to trust in Him, even when we can't see or understand.

So often we live with a strong sense that we understand what God is doing in and through us. In reality, however, most of the time we may not even be close to understanding His purposes. He may be doing things that we cannot see now, nor will we ever see. That is why faithfulness and endurance are essential to ministry.

Jeremiah could not quit the ministry even when he wanted to. The fire in his bones compelled him to continue speaking forth God's Word, even when it cost him so much. We, too, will be compelled in ministry when God's Word burns in our hearts like a fire. We know, too, that God will be our Keeper in all that He chooses for us, that He will reveal the knowledge of His glory through us, and that He will lead us in triumph in His Son. That is enough.

*But thanks be to God, who always leads us in triumphal procession in Christ and through us spreads everywhere the fragrance of the knowledge of him. (2 Corinthians 2:14)*

The psalmist described that same sense of triumph even in the midst of great trials, testings, burdens and disappointments.

*Praise our God, O peoples, let the sound of his praise be heard; he has preserved our lives and kept our feet from slipping. For you, O*

*God, tested us; you refined us like silver. You brought us into prison and laid burdens on our backs. You let men ride over our heads; we went through fire and water, but you brought us to a place of abundance. (Psalms 66:8-12)*

When the psalmist was overwhelmed with his circumstances, it was this truth that sustained him and filled him with hope: God was his keeper, his eternal Father was holding him and protecting his feet from slipping, and he knew that God would not only bring him through this, but out of it all into places of abundance. The Holy Spirit will remind us of these same truths from day to day. God will not only keep us, but for each one of us, the best days are yet ahead! There are places of abundance awaiting you and me in the gracious provisions of our Father.

## REFLECTIONS, COMMITMENTS AND PRAYER

*God, I want to have a passion for the preaching and teaching of the Scriptures. Would You give that to me as a "fire in my bones" as You did with Jeremiah? Would You speak Your Word through me and bring cleansing, healing and life to Your people? And, Father, would You teach me to keep holding onto You when my expectations in the ministry are not fulfilled. Even if You pour out my life in a way that doesn't make any sense to me or the people around me, let me keep trusting You. May Your glory be seen through me, even before the angels.*

*Jesus gave them this answer: "I tell you the truth, the Son can do nothing by himself; he can do only what he sees his Father doing, because whatever the Father does the Son also does."*

*John 5:19*

# 10

## *Jesus: Walking in the Father's Vision*

T he truths that Solomon taught us—everything that God does will endure forever; nothing can be added to it and nothing taken from it—undergirded Jesus' ministry from day to day. If ministry is what God does, and He is the only explanation for its fulfillment, then He desires from us a responsive heart as we walk with Him. Jesus vividly modeled that responsive lifestyle before us and taught us how to walk in the Father's vision and how to participate with Him in His eternal work. Following Jesus' model and relying on His resources are our greatest protection from ministry *burnout*.

### DID JESUS REALLY BATTLE BURNOUT?

We can readily accept the fact that Jesus is our supreme example in preventing *burnout*, but did He Himself struggle with the same vulnerability to lose heart in the ministry? Did He battle with the same destructive forces with which we struggle every day? I believe

225

He did; the writer to the Hebrews makes it clear that Jesus was fully human and suffered temptation just as we do.

*Because he himself suffered when he was tempted, he is able to help those who are being tempted. (Hebrews 2:18)*

As part of His Father's sovereign process for His ministry, Jesus was led into a time of temptation in the wilderness.

*Then Jesus was led by the Spirit into the desert to be tempted by the devil. After fasting forty days and forty nights, he was hungry. (Matthew 4:1,2)*

Jesus had gone without food for forty days and was in a terribly weakened condition physically when He was confronted by the enemy. When we are tired and weak, our great High Priest can help us in times of temptation as the battles become more than we can bear. He has been there and can relate in every way to the things we are experiencing.

The temptations that Jesus faced in the wilderness are the same ones we face daily. Satan tempted Him to satisfy His physical desires outside of the will of God, to seek His identity in His performances rather than in His relationship with His Father, to short cut God's process in His life and ministry, and to bypass the cross in pursuit of the glory of this world. We will deal with these further in the next chapter.

Did Jesus ever come to the very edge? Did He ever teeter on the precipice of *burnout*? Did He ever come to the place where He simply was unable to continue except for the supernatural, sustaining grace of His Father? I believe that in the Garden of Gethsemane, Jesus reached this point of no return. When He was in the garden, Jesus' soul was overwhelmed with the cup that His Father had set before Him. Bearing the sins of mankind alone and being cut off from the face of His Father for the first time since eternity seemed more than He could bear. Christ asked His disciples to keep watch with Him while He prayed.

> *He took Peter and the two sons of Zebedee along with him, and he began to be sorrowful and troubled. Then he said to them, "My soul is overwhelmed with sorrow to the point of death. Stay here and keep watch with me." (Matthew 26:37,38)*

In the overwhelming sorrow that He faced, Jesus asked His Father if the cup of His wrath that the Son must drink could be passed from Him.

> *Going a little farther, he fell with his face to the ground and prayed, "My Father, if it is possible, may this cup be taken from me. Yet not as I will, but as you will." (Matthew 26:39)*

As Luke records this terrible battle in the garden, he tells us that an angel ministered strength to Jesus during those hours.

> *An angel from heaven appeared to him and strengthened him. And being in anguish, he prayed more earnestly, and his sweat was like drops of blood falling to the ground. (Luke 22:43,44)*

It is possible that apart from His Father's gracious provision for Him during this time, God the Son could have been physically crushed under the weight of what had been set before Him. Apart from God's sovereign protection, plan and timing, Christ may have died before the cross if God had not sustained Him. Jesus knows about *burnout.* He knows what it is to be on the verge of losing heart. The image of legions of angels (Matt. 26:53) coming to His rescue must have been a very real temptation to Him as He faced the cross.

We do not face a struggle as deep as that in our daily ministries, but as we continue to look at Jesus' ministry, He also faced all of the temptations and difficulties that confront us. God's gracious provisions are also there for us. The way in which Jesus walked through these times provides a visual example for us, and the power of His life within us enables us to walk as He did.

## What Do We See God Doing?

How do we avoid *burnout*? Jesus' ministry, as revealed in the gospel of John, provides the answer. The Jews were persecuting Christ for healing on the Sabbath:

> *Jesus said to them, "My Father is always at his work to this very day, and I, too, am working." (John 5:17)*

"My Father is always working, and I, too, am working" is Jesus' response to the legalists. It is the Son's view of His Father and the way He saw Himself in relationship to God and what He was doing that set our Lord free to minister in a responsive lifestyle. Jesus had only three years to prepare a small group of men for a work that would last for all eternity, yet we sense no pressure in Him to "get on with it" and finish the job. Jesus lived with an awareness of the Father's sovereign timing in His life and ministry, and with the knowledge that God was doing something through Him as part of a vast eternal plan. Thus, Jesus learned to watch and see what the Father was doing and then enter into God's everlasting work.

> *Jesus gave them this answer: "I tell you the truth, the Son can do nothing by himself; he can do only what he sees his Father doing, because whatever the Father does the Son also does." (John 5:19)*

We often become totally consumed with what we are doing and we lose any sense of what God desires to do with us and among us. Our eyes so quickly become focused on, even blinded by, what we must accomplish, and at times we are oblivious to what God is doing and what His purposes are for us and our people.

I would love to see a church board come together for its monthly

228

meeting and, as they look around the table at one another, ask these questions: "What do we see God doing? What is He doing in our church? What is God doing in our community? What is He doing around the world? How can we participate in what He is doing?" I would love to see a church come together at their annual congre - gational meeting and ask these same questions! However, we do not ask these questions very often because we have our own agendas. Of course, for board meetings we all use agendas which can be valuable organizational tools in the context of seeking the Lord. However, our vulnerability is when we have so much to do and so many places to go that we cannot see beyond them. Our eyes become filled up with what we are doing so that we have no sense at all of what God is doing.

Even our prayer times as leaders sometimes reflect this failed ministry lifestyle. We keep asking God to enter into what we are doing. We want Him to bless our plans, to give them life, and to make them happen. Jesus did not do that. Rather than asking the Father to enter into what He was doing, He desired to enter into His Father's eternal work.

When I was young in the ministry and encouraging believers with one-to-one discipleship, I was asked by a friend to help begin a new church near the area where we lived. Pat had come to know the Lord through the ministry of Peninsula Bible Church in Palo Alto, California while he was a student at Stanford University and had grown deeply in his understanding of the Christian life and ministry there under Pastor Ray Stedman.

A short time after we had begun the work of this new church, I was invited to teach a seminar in the same area as Peninsula Bible Church. I suggested to Pat that he accompany me on the trip and that we try to have lunch with Ray Stedman and get his counsel about our new church work. We were able to arrange lunch with this gracious, wise and experienced man of God. During our time together, we talked about our hopes and dreams and our great plans for this new work. We were really taken aback by his first statement: "Don't expect anything to happen for at least seven years. Plan for the long term!"

However, there was one question that I had been especially eager to ask Ray. When there was a pause in the conversation, I said, "How do you give someone a hunger for the Word of God? How do you stimulate within a person a desire to grow in the Lord?" I will never forget his answer! "You cannot do that," Ray said. "Only God can give a person a hunger for Himself and His Word. All you can do is teach the Scriptures faithfully and shepherd the people with His heart, but keep your eyes open. When you see God working in someone's life, jump in there and start fanning the flames as quickly as you can. Spend time with them and keep encouraging them in every way possible."

## GOD IS THE INITIATOR IN MINISTRY

That is precisely the way Jesus walked in ministry from day to day. Why did Jesus watch to see what God was doing? Like Solomon, He knew that only the things that God does will endure forever. Because of that understanding and because Jesus had been sent to do His Father's will, Christ saw the Father as the initiative in His life and ministry and Himself as living in a responsive relationship with Him.

> "By myself I can do nothing; I judge only as I hear, and my judgment is just, for I seek not to please myself but him who sent me." (John 5:30)

Jesus had willfully limited Himself when He came to earth. He never ceased being God in His Person and nature, but He laid down many of His prerogatives. He had come to do His Father's will and to please Him in every way. This is a theme that the apostle John fully develops in his gospel.

> *Jesus answered, "My teaching is not my own. It comes from him who sent me. If anyone chooses to do God's will, he will find out whether my teaching comes from God or whether I speak on my own." (John 7:16,17)*

Christ knew that He had been sent by the Father to speak His words and to do His will. Jesus made this statement in the context of questions by the Jews about His level of understanding though He did not have their level of religious education. He then drew the parallel between knowing and submitting. It is the one who subjects Himself to the will of God that is able to discern the source of truth; the person who does his own will lives in darkness.

> *So Jesus said, "When you have lifted up the Son of Man, then you will know that I am the one I claim to be and that I do nothing on my own but speak just what the Father has taught me. The one who sent me is with me; he has not left me alone, for I always do what pleases him." (John 8:28,29)*

As the Jews continued to question the Lord about His origins and His message, Jesus told them that there would come a time when they would understand that His claims to be the Messiah were valid. In His death at Calvary, Jesus would be revealed as the Son of God and the Savior of the world. Christ again affirmed His submission to His Father's will and to the message God had entrusted to Him. Only in this way could He walk in the Father's vision and be preserved from *burnout* in the process.

## A VESSEL FOR THE FATHER'S LIFE

Perhaps the clearest and fullest summary statement of the way Christ saw His relationship with His Father and His ministry came just before the Upper Room Discourse, those last hours that He spent with His disciples before the cross.

> *"For I did not speak of my own accord, but the Father who sent me commanded me what to say and how to say it. I know that his command leads to eternal life. So whatever I say is just what the Father has told me to say." (John 12:49,50)*

Jesus was sent to earth with a message entrusted by His Father. However, He was not only commissioned with *what* to say but with *how* to say it. Christ was a steward of not only the Father's words but the Father's heart. Saying the same things that the Father says, in the same way that He says them was the mission of the Lord Jesus. Christ knew that His Father would bring life out of His own obedience as well as out of the words that He spoke. That knowl - edge motivated Him with a great sense of stewardship in His message before the disciples, the multitudes and the religious leaders.

> *"Don't you believe that I am in the Father, and that the Father is in me? The words I say to you are not just my own. Rather, it is the Father, living in me, who is doing his work." (John 14:10)*

As the apostle John progressively revealed the ministry lifestyle of Christ, he pictured for us the depth of intimacy He shared with the Father—"I am in the Father, and the Father is in me"—and the way in which He saw Himself as a vessel for the Father's words and works. "The words I am speaking are my Father's words, and the works I am doing are my Father's works." We, too, need to see ourselves as vessels through whom the Father is speaking His words and fulfilling His works. It is His life and His ministry that flow through us.

## SAYING "YES" AND SAYING "NO"

What was the fruit of Christ's ministry lifestyle, that of watching to see what God was doing and then entering into His eternal work? It gave Him the freedom to walk responsively before His Father and to give Himself freely to those the Father was bringing to Him. There was an evident spontaneity and flexibility to Jesus' ministry that is very refreshing to all of us whose lives are rigidly scheduled down to the very last minute! We see Jesus stopping on the way from Judea to Galilee to talk to a woman at a well bringing redemption to her life and healing to her heart. At the same time, of course, He is also teaching the disciples, and us, about racism, about God's sovereignty in salvation, and about the meaning of true worship!

Jesus also had the freedom to raise a widow's son while He was on the way to Nain, and God caused the news about Him to spread throughout Judea. When Jesus was passing through Jericho, Zacchaeus wanted to see Him, and Jesus responded by inviting Himself to Zacchaeus' house! At the same time He teaches us about genuine repentance and the fact that God is not a respecter of persons. In a crowd He could be touched by a woman with a hemorrhage and stop to talk with her. However, watching each moment to see what God was doing did not mean saying "yes" to every invitation and opportunity that came Jesus' way.

> *Now there were some Greeks among those who went up to worship at the Feast. They came to Philip, who was from Bethsaida in Galilee, with a request. "Sir," they said, "we would like to see Jesus." Philip went to tell Andrew; Andrew and Philip in turn told Jesus. (John 12:20-22)*

Picture this incredible scene with me. Some Greeks who had come to worship at the Passover Feast had heard about Jesus and asked Philip if they could see Him. The request seemed to go through the channels of the disciples until it came to Jesus Himself.

We would expect Him to say, "Well, bring them right in!" Surely this was the purpose of His coming, for men to be introduced to Him. Could He have any greater heart's desire?

> *Jesus replied, "The hour has come for the Son of Man to be glorified." (John 12:23)*

There is no indication in the Scriptures that these men ever met Jesus. Because He lived with such a keen sense of His Father's sovereign timing in His life and ministry, there was a time for men to be introduced to Him and then a time to set His face to Jerusalem and focus on the cross. We, too, must learn to watch and see what God is doing and to enter into His eternal work. That will some - times mean saying "yes" to people and experiences that we did not plan on, and "no" to some things that may be expected by us and those around us.

Often the fear of displeasing those who desire something of us keeps us from saying "no." Sometimes we are manipulated by guilt from our own hearts or from the enemy or from others as we say "yes" when we should be saying "no." Our desires to please people become more important than asking the question, "What is God leading me to do?" When we become need-motivated and keep saying "yes" to the requests of others, we often develop attitudes of anger, resentment and bitterness as the expectations overwhelm our resources. At this point we are very vulnerable to burning out. In my own desire to care for people with a servant's heart, I have often found myself so focused on their needs and desires that I lose a sense of what God has called me to give them. In the end, I am not only empty and exhausted, but also deeply frustrated.

## MINISTRY: A MARRIAGE OF FOUR VISIONS

If we desire to walk in the Father's vision, we cannot be driven by the needs of people or even by our own dreams. How do we discern the Father's vision in the midst of all that we bring to ministry and all that people desire of us in the process? Vision is critical in ministry, but, at the same time, it can be one of the most trouble - some and vulnerable places for us as we seek to do the Father's will.

One of the Scriptures that we as pastors and leaders often quote to our people is this well-known verse from the book of Proverbs:

*Where there is no vision the people perish ...*
*(Proverbs 29:18a KJV)*

Somehow we have come to link leadership with vision; a great leader is a visionary who will move his people on to fulfill great things. When we talk about vision, our eyes often become filled with the things we desire to accomplish and the hopes and dreams we have been nurturing for years. Yet, when God talks about vision, He desires our eyes and our hearts to be filled up with who He is and what He is doing.

Jesus was a visionary, but none of His visions or dreams began with Himself; He was always seeking His Father and watching to see what He was doing. The Father was always the initiative as well as the purpose for everything the Son did. He had no dreams whatsoever for what He desired to accomplish of Himself but only to enter into what the Father was doing. He lived every moment to please His Father.

We desperately need vision in God's Church today! However, we do not need any more dreamers with great plans to build exciting programs for ministry such as this world has never seen. We need visions of God. We need men and women who hunger to see His holiness as revealed to Isaiah. We need to see the glory of God that He showed to Ezekiel, the sovereignty He taught to Job, the sufficiency with which God moved Moses, the vision of His faithfulness with which He began Ezekiel's ministry, the vision of

His life-giving Word that God gave to Jeremiah, and the view of Christ's Lordship with which the apostle Paul lived each day.

## Our Visions and Dreams

Vision is one of the real trouble points of ministry and one of the areas in which we are most vulnerable to losing heart. As is often the case, a young man or woman will begin thinking and dreaming of future ministries as he or she experiences solid confirmation of God's call. Through seminary a man's dreams will be fed by his study of the Scriptures, by many helpful tools for ministry, by the examples of godly men and women before him, and by the models of great preachers and teachers.

Afterwards while serving as an assistant pastor or pastoring a small country or inner city church, these dreams grow. "Someday I will be in the place where I will have the experience and the supportive environment to do the things that God put into my heart." Of course, it is wonderful to have dreams, and they often flow out of God's stirring in our hearts, but if we hold onto them with a strong sense of ownership, we are vulnerable.

Later the call comes from the larger suburban church with a great location, a good facility, and a solid board. It is just the place to put into practice the things this young man has learned and dreamed about!

## The Visions of Those to Whom We Are Called

This man is not the only one who has dreams for his ministry; the people to whom he has been called have visions and dreams, too. These are called expectations! For years they have been saying, "We have a beautiful building. We are in a wonderful, growing community. We have excellent leadership. We have a great resource of young couples. If only we had the right pastor—a great preacher and a strong leader—this church would really take off!" Now, here comes the man through whom their dreams will be fulfilled.

236

On a recent trip to the Philippines, I was invited to teach a seminar in a local church on "Developing a Heart for Ministry." During the teaching, we focused on a great view of a sovereign God, on how ministry is what God does, and the way in which we can rest in Him and the power of his Word and His Spirit to fulfill His will. We also talked about aggressive responsiveness, that is the way in which God has called us to faithfulness, to work with all of our hearts to accomplish in His strength what He has set before us.

I had taught in this fine, young church on earlier trips to the Philippines, but it had not grown as the founding missionaries had hoped. This time, however, they had a new pastor. I enjoyed meeting him and sharing with him in the fellowship of the ministry that day. A few days later I had the opportunity to speak to a group of pastors and missionaries from his denomination. During a time of ques-tions and discussion, he began to talk about what had just taken place in his heart.

He shared that he had been a professor in a Bible college in the Philippines. He loved his ministry and felt that God was using him in a significant way, thus he had no thoughts or plans to go anywhere else. However, the leaders of this church asked him to become the pastor of their young fellowship with all of its potential. They had, in fact, been thinking, "We have a great location in an upper class area. We have many attractive young couples. If we only had the right pastor, the church would really grow."

After much prayer and persuasion by the elders, this young man felt led of the Lord to leave his very fruitful ministry at the Bible college and become the church's new pastor. In the months since he had come, rather than the church exploding in attendance as everyone "knew" it would, they had lost 25% of their people. The heart of this young man was crushed. He was overwhelmed with the pressure of "growing" this church. As he opened his heart to us at that meeting, he told us how disappointed he was in himself because he thought he would do better. His leaders had said, "We are disappointed in you; we thought you would do better." His own wife had come to him and said, "I am disappointed in you. I thought you would do better."

Then he told us that during this weekend of ministry, God had lifted from him the pressure of building this church and of making the ministry happen. He said, "I want to share with you the commitment I made this weekend. I will teach the Word faithfully and shepherd my people with God's heart the best I know how, but I will no longer take upon myself the pressure for all of the responsibility of this ministry. I will trust God to do what only He can do."

It is not only our dreams that cause us to be vulnerable and to give up in the ministry. The dreams of others also bring us great pressure. Many of our pastors are losing heart because they are not measuring up to the expectations of their people. Following Jesus' ministry lifestyle of "watching to see what God is doing" and entering into His eternal work is our greatest protection from burning out under the expectations of those whom God has given us in ministry.

## The Visions of Our Peers

As if the pressures of our church members were not enough, we often need to cope with the dreams of our peers. In our modern ministry culture, we have tools available for building ministries that people hardly dreamed of a few years ago. We have methods and insights, principles and mechanisms that seem foolproof. If we present the message in the right way, within the right environment, with the right level of acceptability, with the proper comfort zones, then we can achieve the level of desired response. We truly believe that, as was stated in the movie *Field of Dreams*, "if we build it, they will come."

I have heard from many pastors of small churches who find it very difficult to attend their denominational meetings or even to meet with a small group of fellow pastors. Rather than being built up and encouraged, these times often cause them to lose heart. It seems that there is no possibility any more for a small church to be healthy and to have a substantial ministry, for the pastors are sent the message, "If your church is not growing numerically, there is something wrong with you or your message or your methods. If you are doing it right, your church will grow." In North America we are future-oriented pragmatists who are committed to progress and who expect growth. We are convinced that "if we do these things that are proven to work, then we will achieve the success that we desire." However, God does not fit into that mindset. As we have seen in other places in our study, many pastors are losing their ability to endure under these pressures to produce.

Another kind of peer pressure that can cause us to lose heart is conflict of visions for the work. This happened to me a few years ago. Our work of discipleship, publishing and seminars had been going well, and we sensed God's blessing on the ministry. Interna - tional opportunities had begun to open, and we could all sense the organization's great potential in the future. However, there seemed to be financial limitations on what we were able to do. God was meeting our needs, but there was always the underlying thought, "If we only had more money, just think of what we would be able to do."

During this time, one of my closest friends, who was pastoring a suburban Chicago church, had one of the wealthy elders suggest to him and to us that our ministry come under the authority of his church, and they would completely fund the ministry of Leadership Resources. This seemed like a perfect solution to our need for finances for the growing Third World doors God was opening to us. Several of our board and staff felt we should do this, but I was concerned. I was deeply involved in the ministry of our home church, and this change would necessitate all of our staff members joining this new church. I did not feel that money was a good enough reason to leave a church, and when I thought about this wealthy elder, I was also wary about the relationship between money, power and control. My own pastor, Bill Johnson, wisely counseled me, "Bill, God will never allow you to be in a situation where you do not have to depend on Him."

As time went on, the board and staff members who felt that we should respond to this opportunity and move to this new church became more and more convinced that this was God's leading for our ministry. However, concerns continued to grow in my own heart, and I felt I could not leave the church where God had placed me. It did not seem to me that my brothers in the organization could hear what I was saying. In the midst of this pressure-filled situation, I lost heart. I quit. I resigned from my position. My co-workers on the board and staff had no idea that I was in this kind of trouble, and I didn't either. I felt that I was caught in a whirlpool, being pulled down, and I didn't know how to handle the pressure. I never would have guessed that I was that vulnerable to losing heart and burning out. I never saw myself as a quitter. My co-workers had no intentions of opposing me to such a degree that I would give up. Their desires were completely honorable; they only saw the good of the ministry as their goal. I became caught in the confusion, the pressures and the expectations, and my strength and hope were drained away in the process. I know that if "my eyes were on the Lord and I was trusting in Him," I never would have quit, but that is the nature of *burnout*. We often become over-whelmed before we can sort it all out.

God brought us through that time. He called me back, but

it took months for my heart to be restored. He met us and healed our hearts together. We received strength from the Lord and encouragement from each other. I often teach, "We can go through anything together; as we respond the way God teaches us and enables us, our relationships will be even stronger than they were before." I know that is true because God not only kept my heart, He kept our relationships. That was several years go, and we are all still working together, com - mitted to each other, and loving one another more deeply as the days go by.

### God's Vision for Our Ministries

We, our people, and our peers are not the only ones who have dreams and visions for our ministry. God has dreams as well. From the foundation of the world, He has prepared His works for us to do.

> For we are God's workmanship, created in Christ Jesus to do good works, which God prepared in advance for us to do. (Ephesians 2:10)

The same God who has called us and prepared us for ministry has prepared ministry for us! Jesus said, "The Father living in me is doing His work." God desires to work in us as well as through us. When our eyes are on Him and what He is doing, we are free to walk in that which He has set before us. May God give us the grace each day to ask, "What does God desire to do in my life today? What is He doing in the lives of those around me and in the building of His Church throughout the world? How can I, like Jesus, walk in the Father's vision?"

## HOW DO WE LEARN TO SEE?

How do we learn to see what God is doing and then walk with the Father in His vision for our ministries? Once again, Jesus' model teaches us how to walk with God in the ministries He has set before us. We see an example of the way in which Jesus experienced this as He chose His twelve apostles.

> *One of those days Jesus went out to a mountainside to pray, and spent the night praying to God. When morning came, he called his disciples to him and chose twelve of them, whom he also designated apostles: ... (Luke 6:12,13)*

## Prayer

Christ spent the entire night in prayer, and *then* He chose His twelve apostles. Jesus was not talking to His Father all night; He was listening. Jesus knew that His Father had far more to say to Him than He had to say to His Father! There were perhaps as many as several hundred people who had begun to follow Jesus by this time. Christ knew that this was the Father's timing to focus His ministry on a handful of men and prepare them for the work of building His Church. In those hours of prayer, the Son of God was seeking His Father's heart for those whom God would entrust to Him with the work of preparing His own Bride. During those hours God was saying, "It is Matthew and Thomas, James and John, Andrew and Peter." "Peter?" "Yes, Peter!, and...."

It was through prayer, intimacy and communion with His Father that Jesus learned to see what God was doing. Coming before His Father continually with a listening, sensitive, responsive heart was the environment in which Christ walked in the works prepared for Him from the foundation of the world. Many of us struggle with a lack of direction and without any sense at all of what God desires to do in and through us. Could this be a reflection of our prayer lives, of our lack of intimacy and communion with God, of a failure to come consistently with a listening and responsive heart? Just a cursory reading of Jesus' prayer life revealed in the gospels de - mands that we examine ourselves in this area. What is the level of intimacy that we are experiencing with God in prayer? Are we keeping prayer diaries and consistently bringing our lives, families and congregations before the Lord?

## The Scriptures

Jesus also learned to see what God was doing by studying the Scriptures. At the beginning of His public ministry, He went to Nazareth, His home town. He stood in the synagogue on the Sabbath and read this Scripture from the scroll of Isaiah.

> *"The Spirit of the Lord is on me, because he has anointed me to preach good news to the poor. He has sent me to proclaim freedom for the prisoners and recovery of sight for the blind, to release the oppressed, to proclaim the year of the Lord's favor."* (Luke 4:18,19)

When He had finished reading, He began to teach them by saying, "Today this Scripture is fulfilled in your hearing" (vs. 21). Jesus did not come to earth "pre-programmed." He had to learn what God had for Him, just as we do. The Holy Spirit had taught the Son of God what His ministry would be about as He studied the Scriptures. As He read and searched the prophets, God taught His Son that the Old Testament writings were about Him (Luke 24:25-27) and that His ministry would be to the poor, the prisoners, the blind and the oppressed.

If we desire to see what God is doing, we, too, must begin with the Scriptures, because the priorities of our great, unchanging God have been established from eternity. It is in the Word of God that we learn the purposes that fill our Father's heart: His holiness exalted (Isaiah 6:1-4), His glory filling the earth (Habakkuk 2:14), His Church being built (Matthew 16:18), and His compassion and justice seen toward the poor, the hungry and the oppressed (Isaiah

58:6-12). God will surely not lead us into anything less than that which has filled His heart from the beginning.

**Our Spiritual Gifts**

Working in the area of our spiritual gifts is also a means of "watching to see what God is doing." The way in which Christ has equipped us for ministry is part of His protection against our losing heart.

> But to each one of us grace has been given as Christ apportioned it. This is why it says: "When he ascended on high, he led captives in his train and gave gifts to men." (Ephesians 4:7,8)

Our spiritual gifts are best discerned through service rather than by the multitude of paper tests that are available today. God reveals the way in which He has designed us to fit into the Body of Christ as we respond to ministry opportunities, receive the affirma - tion of the leaders that God has entrusted to us, and see people's responses to the work He is doing through us.

We seem to have a sense of urgency in "discovering" our spiritual gifts, as though they are some hidden treasure that will unlock a new and vibrant ministry. Perhaps a more realistic understanding of the apostle Paul's teaching on gifts to the churches at Rome (Romans 12:1-8) and Corinth (1 Corinthians 12-14) is that he is describing to the readers why the Church functions as it does, rather than setting before us a set of ministry slots that we must somehow fit into. As we respond to ministry needs and serve as we have opportunity, God will steadily reveal the way He has planned to use us. Then, as we focus our hearts and our resources in those areas, joy and fruitfulness sustain us along the way.

**Keeping Our Eyes Open**

Like Jesus, too, we must live moment by moment with the awareness that "God is always working" and realize that God might do with us something other than what we had planned for the next

hour or week or worship service. Often by watching the circum -
stances that God in His sovereignty allows to develop, ministries
we are involved in will be redirected for periods of time. Sometimes
a crisis in our family or in a church family will cause us to lay aside
our plans for days, weeks, or even years in order to be available
for those needs. If we do not see this as God's sovereignty at work
in our lives and ministries, we will be greatly frustrated.

"Watching to see what God is doing" transformed the nature of
this ministry. For the first seven years, this was a work of "one-to-
one" discipleship. We spent hours each week with people, person -
ally encouraging them in the Scriptures and their walk with the
Lord. Then, God began to open opportunities for us to teach these
same truths to churches in seminars. When we saw the great
response of churches, we saw, too, that this is what God was leading
us to do, and the one-to-one work was preparation for what He had
set before us.

Sometimes, too, God will bring new opportunities for service,
such as a community-wide evangelistic outreach or an invitation to
give ourselves in an area in which God has equipped us. For a
period of time this may be a focus on families or on those in hurting
relationships. Perhaps an area of need or weakness will be revealed
in the church, and God will use that to lead us to a new preaching
series or to give a major portion of our time to meet that need.

### Listening to Our Leaders

Paul taught the church at Ephesus that the ministry belongs to
the people (Eph. 4:11,12) rather than to the professionals, and God
has raised us up to equip them for the work. If we believe this, we
will allow ministry to arise from God's people rather than hold
tightly to a concept of the pastoral staff or church board being the
sole source of direction and fulfillment of the work.

At our home church right now, our pastors and elders are

praying about a new direction for the work of our elder board. Rather than seeing this board as an august gathering of mature saints who meet to make major decisions for the church and try to put out the fires that keep flaring up, we are praying about the heart of the ministry as shepherding the people. It sounds revolutionary, doesn't it! How would this look? We do not know for sure, but perhaps we may spend our board meeting times in the homes of our people praying with them rather than in a room at the church making decisions about them. At least it will mean more availability and contact with the members of the Body, hearing their hearts, bearing their hurts with them, asking about their marriages and children, and sharing our Father's love.

The freedom to be open to a new direction in ministry grows out of the heart of our senior pastor, Pat Peglow, and his willingness to listen to his leaders, watching what God is doing. At the same time, I must say that our elders see our pastor as the primary leader in the ministry and are responsive, even submissive, to him. We recognize that he has been called of God to be the primary keeper and developer of the vision for the ministry God has entrusted to us. Together, we seek to follow Jesus' model of walking in the Father's vision.

If we are committed to listening to our leaders, they will surely have major input into every significant decision concerning the direction of the ministries in which we are involved. This will undoubtedly include whether to leave our present church, or when to leave and pursue another ministry. We so often tend to see ourselves as "lone rangers" and make major decisions on our own. This attitude leads to a terrible sense of aloneness and is a prime environment for *burnout*. As an expression of our submission to God and to our leaders we will include them in the process and will seek their counsel, prayers and direction. I work for a "para - church" ministry, teaching within the greater Body of Christ, but I see myself under the authority of my elders and this ministry as an expression of our local church.

## Our Hearts Before the Lord

In watching to see what God is doing and seeking His direction for our lives and ministries, we cannot be reminded often enough that the heart with which we come before Him is always the major issue. Our ability to "discover God's will," or to figure things out and to discern correctly in each situation is never the issue. God spoke to His people about this very truth through the prophet Isaiah.

The context of this Scripture is the hardhearted rebellion of God's children in the face of His call to see Him, to trust Him, and to find in Him alone all of their rest, their strength and their salvation. For those who seek Him with a whole heart, God says this:

> *Whether you turn to the right or to the left, your ears will hear a voice behind you, saying, "This is the way; walk in it."* (Isaiah 30:21)

That is a wonderful description of the sense of God's presence that we need from day to day and the assurance of His direction. When we are honest about it, even the wisest and the most experienced of us would never "get it right" when we depend on ourselves. The heart with which we come before the Lord is the most important aspect of discerning His leading for our lives and ministries. For those who come before the Father with responsive hearts, there is no possibility in all of the world that they will ever miss anything that God has for them.

## JESUS IS THE LIFE SOURCE

This, then, is the way in which Jesus functioned in His life and His ministry. He was submitted to the Father's will and desired to please Him continually. He watched to see what God was doing and walked in His Father's vision. He spoke the Father's words with His Father's heart. He saw Himself as a vessel for the Father's life. If ours, like that of the Lord Jesus, is to become a responsive ministry lifestyle, our focus must be on God and His eternal work. Our vision cannot become locked into our own dreams, plans and objectives. We cannot allow ourselves to be limited by the visions of our peers or crushed under the expectations of our people. The Lord Jesus not only modeled this lifestyle before us; He empowers us to serve Him in this way.

> *"Remain in me, and I will remain in you. No branch can bear fruit by itself; it must remain in the vine. Neither can you bear fruit unless you remain in me. I am the vine; you are the branches. If a man remains in me and I in him, he will bear much fruit; apart from me you can do nothing." (John 15:4,5)*

After Christ pictured Himself as the vine and His Father as the gardener, He called His disciples to remain, or abide, in Him. In John 14:10 Jesus had said, "The Father living in Me is doing His work." Now He is telling His disciples, as well as us, "My life living in you will do My work." The Son of God is revealing to His followers the key to fruitfulness in ministry: an intimate, responsive, shared life relationship with Him. He is calling His disciples to take their focus off the fruit and place it on their relationship with Him. There is nothing within them that can produce that which only God can do. Thus, Jesus says to you and me, "Come to Me; share My life. Everything that we both desire will flow out of you in abundance!"

> *"I am the vine; you are the branches. If a man remains in me and I in him, he will bear much fruit; apart from me you can do nothing." (John 15:5)*

Jesus is describing Himself to the disciples as the "life source." It is in relationship with Him that they will produce fruit. Apart from Him, whatever they do will come to nothing. In John 14, Jesus had taught His disciples about the ministry of the Holy Spirit whom He would send in His Name. It was the Holy Spirit who fulfilled these truths in the disciples, and He will through you and me as well.

We will look further into the resources of Christ within us as we study the apostle Paul's ministry. We cannot be reminded too often to keep our focus on our relationship with Christ as the means by which God fulfills His will through us. When Jesus' responsive ministry lifestyle becomes our own and His indwelling life our resource, we become vessels for God's words, His works and His life. As He fulfills through us those things which fill His heart, He will sustain us from day to day.

## REFLECTIONS, COMMITMENTS AND PRAYER

*Father, I confess that I have often become consumed with my own vision, plans and goals for ministry, and in these times I have lost sight of what You are doing. In other times, I have deeply bought into the expectations of my people and my peers as well. I have allowed Your vision for me to be supplanted by my own dreams and the expectations of others, and I have experienced the pres - sure and failure of these choices. Would You teach me to focus the eyes of my heart on You, to watch and see what You are doing, and then to walk in Your vision for me and my ministry? Would You enable me to live responsively before You and to draw on the resources of Christ each day? Please protect me from any confidence in myself or my plans, and make me a vessel for Your life.*

*For in Christ all the fullness of the Deity lives in bodily form,
and you have been given fullness in Christ,...*

Colossians 2:9,10a

# 11

## *Paul: Finishing Well*

The Lord Jesus is our supreme model in battling *burnout*. His ministry lifestyle is the example we must follow if we would "finish well" in the life and work that God has set before us. Alongside the Son of God, the apostle Paul vividly illustrates for us God's ability to sustain His servants in the face of even the greatest obstacles in the work that He has entrusted to us. When we study Paul's ministry, we see that he consistently followed Jesus' model.

From Paul we learn that even the most devastating ministry experiences cannot destroy those whom God has called and that the resources of Christ's indwelling life empower us in all that God has set before us. We see, too, the fullness of Christ, which is able to satisfy us on every level in every way, and the marks of finishing well in the work God has entrusted to us.

251

## CONFLICTS WITHOUT, FEARS WITHIN

One of the things that enables Paul to be such a powerful example for us is that he faced all of the things with which we battle day after day. Paul was confronted with divisions on his ministry team, religious zealots who continually sought to undermine his message, and political systems that sought to destroy him and the gospel he preached. He faced devastating afflictions and overwhelming circumstances. The churches to whom he ministered were caught up in politics among the leaders, struggled with doctrinal errors, and continually lost their sense of identity and their vision for ministry. He fought inner battles as well, such as confusion, weakness, depression and a great sense of inadequacy. Added to this was a work load that would destroy anyone whose own strength was his enablement, and the result is a ministry in which *burnout* is inevitable unless God meets us there.

Sometimes our images of the great men and women of the Scriptures do not permit us to see them in reality, but the truth is that Paul was brutally honest about himself and his circumstances. This is the way he describes his heart to the Corinthians as he came to Macedonia:

> *For when we came into Macedonia, this body of ours had no rest, but we were harassed at every turn—conflicts on the outside, fears within. But God, who comforts the downcast, comforted us by the coming of Titus, ... (2 Corinthians 7:5,6)*

The New American Standard Bible translation states, "But God who comforts the depressed." This is the apostle Paul speaking! Did he experience depression? Could it be that, just as we, his soul was sometimes overwhelmed as he served the Lord? The descrip-tion of what happened to him as he was led by the Spirit of God into Macedonia enables us, even in the most challenging ministry situations, to identify with him. His body had no rest; he was at the point of physical exhaustion; he was harassed; Paul faced conflicts, fears and depression at every turn. How does anyone get through this?

> *... and not only by his coming but also by the comfort you had given him. He told us about your longing for me, your deep sorrow, your ardent concern for me, so that my joy was greater than ever. (2 Corinthians 7:7)*

The comfort of a brother and the love of a church were used of God to sustain Paul in these days. He was not only able to endure through this time but also to experience joy in these difficult days. In fact he said, "My joy was greater than ever!"

## THE COMFORT OF A BROTHER

As I was preparing this material, I visited with a good friend who pastors a large international church. When I described to him the work that I was doing in developing a book on "battling *burnout* in the ministry," he shocked me by saying, "In some circumstances it is not possible to prevent *burnout* except by getting out!" Some situations are almost designed for a pastor to lose heart if he remains. Of course, God can keep our hearts in any circumstances, but it is no admission of failure for a leader to conclude that he has had all he can handle in one place and to be sensitive to the Lord's leading if He might open another door. In making decisions like this, the pattern of "watching to see what God is doing" that we see in the life of our Lord Jesus is foundational to discerning God's leading. Listening to the counsel of our elders and maintaining a pure heart before the Lord are also essential in this process for our motives and decisions to be right and to glorify the Lord.

My friend was pastoring a multi-cultural church with a myriad of expectations from his people. The expatriates came and went, sometimes sent by their companies for only a few months or for a couple of years. He would develop friendships and then those people would be transferred. The loss and the sense of aloneness were sometimes more than he could bear. God also gave him very close friends among the nationals, but there were always cultural barriers. Being a highly educated and intellectual congregation, the nationals had very high expectations for his teaching. The needs of the people varied with different cultures, and the demands for his time and expertise were high. The needs of his own family were also a primary concern for his heart. The church had gone through a difficult time before the Lord led him there, and he had worked hard to bring it back to a strong place of prominent ministry. He was tired.

Yet, our Father was able to keep his heart and to sustain him in the ministry. God did this through the support of his leaders and his staff and by means of many other resources—those very truths which we are studying here. One of God's primary tools in this process, however, was the gift of two or three close friends who gave themselves to my brother, even as Titus was there for Paul when he desperately needed comfort and encouragement. If you are in circumstances like this, perhaps one of the places to begin is to ask God to bring a friend who can walk with you closely during these days and who can be a source of needed comfort and encourage - ment.

## MOMENTARY LIGHT AFFLICTIONS

When we think of the pressures, demands and afflictions which would cause us to lose heart in the ministry, we can fully identify with Paul. As he was pressured to defend his apostleship before the church at Corinth, he described some of his day-to-day battles as he served his Lord:

*Are they Hebrews? So am I. Are they Israelites? So am I. Are they Abraham's descendants? So am I. Are they servants of Christ? (I am out of my mind to talk like this.) I am more. I have worked much harder, been in prison more frequently, been flogged more severely, and been exposed to death again and again. Five times I received from the Jews the forty lashes minus one.*
*(2 Corinthians 11:22-24)*

Paul was put into the position of comparing himself before the Corinthian church with those who were "super-apostles" in their eyes. His heritage, his background and his calling were the same as theirs, but his work much more difficult.

*Three times I was beaten with rods, once I was stoned, three times I was shipwrecked, I spent a night and a day in the open sea, I have been constantly on the move. I have been in danger from rivers, in danger from bandits, in danger from my own countrymen, in danger from Gentiles; in danger in the city, in danger in the country, in danger at sea; and in danger from false brothers. (2 Corinthians 11:25,26)*

His incredible beatings and imprisonments and his being ex-posed to death over and over again are hard enough to read about, much less to experience. Five times he received the standard Roman punishment of the thirty-nine lashes from which many prisoners died. The continual dangers grip our hearts with awe as we sense something of the great apostle's ability to endure.

*I have labored and toiled and have often gone without sleep; I have known hunger and thirst and have often gone without food; I have been cold and naked. Besides everything else, I face daily the pressure of my concern for all the churches.*
*(2 Corinthians 11:27,28)*

As Paul summarizes his physical testings, he lays before us an even greater burden. There was another pressure he bore that caused the others to pale in comparison—his daily concern for the churches that God had entrusted to him.

> *Who is weak, and I do not feel weak? Who is led into sin, and I do not inwardly burn? If I must boast, I will boast of the things that show my weakness. (2 Corinthians 11:29,30)*

Paul closely identified with the churches under his care as well as with individual believers. He bore their weaknesses with them, and his heart burned over their sin. It is amazing as we look at this list of persecutions, burdens and battle points that Paul refers to them earlier in his letter as "momentary, light afflictions."

> *Therefore we do not lose heart. Though outwardly we are wasting away, yet inwardly we are being renewed day by day. For our light and momentary troubles are achieving for us an eternal glory that far outweighs them all. (2 Corinthians 4:16,17)*

## THEREFORE WE DO NOT LOSE HEART

This is the second time in this chapter that Paul uses the phrase "we do not lose heart." He began the chapter by telling us that God keeps His shepherds by means of His mercies.

> *Therefore, since through God's mercy we have this ministry, we do not lose heart. (2 Corinthians 4:1)*

Ministry is not the result of any human achievement; ministry is the result of the mercy of God. It is by means of His sustaining mercies which are new every morning that we are kept from day to day. Paul now gives us another expression of God's mercy and that is the ability to see our lives and our ministries from His perspec - tive, to look at our circumstances with eyes fixed on the eternal. Even though our outer persons are breaking down in the midst of the afflictions, God is daily renewing us inwardly. He is using the continuous troubles that we face to develop for us an eternal weight of glory which goes far beyond any pain or loss that we are experiencing now. The ability to see what is eternal in the midst of temporal battles is an expression of God's mercies which hold us when otherwise we could not even last one more day.

> *So we fix our eyes not on what is seen, but on what is unseen. For what is seen is temporary, but what is unseen is eternal. (2 Corinthians 4:18)*

### CHRIST IN YOU, THE HOPE OF GLORY

As we said earlier in this chapter, Paul is a vivid illustration of Jesus' ministry lifestyle. With the eyes to see his life and his ministry from an eternal perspective, he watched to see what God was doing, and he entered into God's eternal work. Jesus said, "The Father living in me is doing His work," and then He called us to "abide in Him." He is our source of life and fruit. Paul saw the indwelling life of Christ as the key to fruitfulness in his own ministry.

To the church at Colossae, Paul wrote of the mystery which had been hidden from past ages and generations but which was now being revealed to the Gentiles.

> *To them God has chosen to make known among the Gentiles the glorious riches of this mystery, which is Christ in you, the hope of glory. (Colossians 1:27)*

Like the apostle Paul, it is not who we are or what we are able to do that is the key to our lives and our ministries; it is *Christ in us!* Who Jesus is, what He is able to do in us and through us by the power of the Holy Spirit, and our responsiveness to Him will be the final determining factors in the fruitfulness of our work. The Person of Christ filling us and overflowing from us is all of our hope in life, in relationships, and in ministry.

## TRIUMPH IN CHRIST

We find in Paul's second Corinthian letter one of the most confi-dence-inspiring statements in God's Word and one that brings us great hope in ministry: God leads us in triumph through His Son! What could anyone tell us that would ease the pressure in ministry like this glorious truth does?

> *But thanks be to God, who always leads us in triumphal proces-sion in Christ and through us spreads everywhere the fragrance of the knowledge of him. (2 Corinthians 2:14)*

God is going before us, and He has already triumphed in His Son! He *always* leads us in triumph! Whatever the circumstances or the battles we face, our Father leads us in triumph through His Son. Everywhere He leads us, the Father is spreading the fragrance of His Son through us. We are following in His victories over His enemies, and God is fulfilling through us those things which are pleasing to Him, revealing Himself to those whom He is calling.

> *For we are to God the aroma of Christ among those who are being saved and those who are perishing. To the one we are the smell of death; to the other, the fragrance of life.*
> *(2 Corinthians 2:15,16a)*

We are the aroma of Christ to God among those who are responding to our walk and message, whether by death or by life. Some are drawn to us, and to God, and receive redemption through the sacrifice of His Son. Others reject both the message and the messenger and perish in their sins. To those responding to the glorious gospel of Christ we are the aroma of life, but to those whose hearts are hardened by their own disobedience and rejection, we are the stench of death.

Just as the Roman soldiers returning victorious from their battles to expand Caesar's kingdom crushed the flower petals his subjects threw in their path, releasing the aroma, we are Christ's aroma to the Father and to those around us. What a description of ministry this is! Ministry is the overflow of God's life as we walk with Him in the works that He has prepared for us from all eternity. In the face of this, Paul is confronted with the one question in ministry that also confronts you and me every day of our lives:

*And who is equal to such a task? (2 Corinthians 2:16b)*

## A New Covenant

After Paul described the integrity and character of his heart before the Lord and before His people, and after the way the Corinthians themselves were the confirmation of his ministry, Paul tells us of the New Covenant relationship in which we serve the Lord. He contrasts the Old Covenant of the Law written with ink on tablets of stone with the New Covenant, written by the Holy Spirit on the hearts of men and women.

> *You show that you are a letter from Christ, the result of our ministry, written not with ink but with the Spirit of the living God, not on tablets of stone but on tablets of human hearts. (2 Corinthians 3:3)*

The apostle now lays before us the basis of his confidence in ministry. Even faced with the question "who is equal to this?", Paul's heart remains confident in the service of His Lord. However, the basis of his confidence is not his background, his education, his eloquence, his persuasiveness, his brilliance, his personality or his strength. All of his competence and all of his adequacy for the ministry come from God.

> *Such confidence as this is ours through Christ before God. Not that we are competent in ourselves to claim anything for ourselves, but our competence comes from God. He has made us*

*competent as ministers of a new covenant—not of the letter but of the Spirit; for the letter kills, but the Spirit gives life. (2 Corinthians 3:4-6)*

Who has had a background, a call, and a preparation for the ministry as substantial as that of the apostle Paul? Yet, none of those gave Paul any basis for confidence in His work. All of His hope was in Christ, His indwelling power and His eternal resources which are sufficient to fulfill that which pleases God and which accomplishes His eternal purposes.

Paul is now experiencing that which Jesus brought to His disciples in His death and resurrection. Christ described this new relationship of life, intimacy and power to His followers on the last night that He spent with them before He went to the cross. At the Last Supper, Jesus took the bread and gave it to His disciples as a remembrance of His body which would be broken for them; then He took the cup and described its significance.

*In the same way, after the supper he took the cup, saying, "This cup is the new covenant in my blood, which is poured out for you." (Luke 22:20)*

To all who will place their faith in Him, Jesus is ushering in a completely new relationship with the Father which will not be based on the Law and how well they are able to keep it. It will not be measured by their performances or by their potential. This New Covenant relationship will flow only out of His redeeming work on Calvary and the power of His life within them to please the Father and for them to be vessels for His eternal works.

Like the apostle Paul, we, too, must reject any confidence in our own abilities in ministry. The truth is that our brilliance, eloquence, personality and strength will not carry us very far in the ministry. They may move people in a shallow sense for a very brief time, but if God accomplishes through us those things which last for eternity, our only basis for hope and confidence will be the eternal resources of the Christ who has called us, who lives within us and who is our sufficiency for all that God has set before us.

## THE PREEMINENCE OF CHRIST

In the first chapter of Paul's letter to the church at Colossae, he sets before us a panoramic view of the Lord Jesus, exalted in His eternal glory and splendor. This is the very Christ who lives in us and who empowers us in all that the Father has given us to do.

*He is the image of the invisible God, ... (Colossians 1:15a)*

Jesus is the God who has become visible. We can see the Father in Him and through Him.

*... the firstborn over all creation. (Colossians 1:15b)*

Jesus is God's most highly exalted reigning Son. He is seated supremely over all that God has created.

*For by him all things were created: ... (Colossians 1:16a)*

Jesus is the source of all that exists. Everything that is has emerged out of His Person.

*... things in heaven and on earth, visible and invisible, whether thrones or powers or rulers or authorities; ... (Colossians 1:16b)*

Jesus is not only the source of physical things, but powers and dominions have come from Him as well.

*... all things were created by him and for him. (Colossians 1:16c)*

Jesus is not only the source of everything that is, but the recipient also. All things will be finalized in Him.

*He is before all things, ... (Colossians 1:17a)*

Jesus is preeminent in all of the realms of earth and heaven, above and before all that exists.

> *... and in him all things hold together. (Colossians 1:17b)*

Jesus is the "glue" in the universe! Everything that is together finds its cohesion in Him alone. It is Christ who binds the planets in their orbits and who holds the molecules within their structures. He is the One who keeps our hearts whole and binds our marriages, our families and our churches together.

> *And he is the head of the body, the church; he is the beginning and the firstborn from among the dead, so that in everything he might have the supremacy. (Colossians 1:18)*

God has designed time and eternity for the single purpose of Jesus, His Son, reigning supreme!

> *For God was pleased to have all his fullness dwell in him, and through him to reconcile to himself all things, whether things on earth or things in heaven, by making peace through his blood, shed on the cross. (Colossians 1:19,20)*

Because all of God's fullness lived in Jesus, through Him the Father was able to reconcile all things to Himself. It was by Christ's blood shed at the cross that peace was purchased with God, the righteous One.

Paul continues with this theme of fullness in the first chapter by writing of the way in which he desires to present the Word of God in its fullness (v. 25) and to present every person complete in Christ. As He closes the chapter, we see a summary statement of the truths that he taught the Corinthians concerning God's ade-quacy in the new covenant.

> *To this end I labor, struggling with all his energy, which so powerfully works in me. (Colossians 1:29)*

We, too, must learn to labor in ministry through the energy of Christ who lives within us or we will burn out. In our brief glimpses of Paul's labors, we can quickly see that he kept an incredible schedule and seemed to work endlessly. From Paul's life we can see that hard work or a heavy schedule are not the primary causes of *burnout*. *Burnout* comes from working in the wrong areas, not watching to see what God is doing, and from working in our own strength. When we place our hope in what we are able to do rather than what Christ is able to do, we will collapse when our resources are depleted.

Paul returns to his message of "fullness" in his second chapter.

*For in Christ all the fullness of the Deity lives in bodily form, and you have been given fullness in Christ, who is the head over every power and authority. (Colossians 2:9,10)*

What a description of who Jesus is—the fullness of God in a physical body! Christ is the fullness of deity in bodily form, and we have been given fullness in Christ! The same Lord Jesus that Paul so wonderfully exalts in his song of worship in Colossians chapter one is the Christ who lives within us and who fills us in every way.

## THE FULLNESS OF CHRIST IN PAUL

What does it mean to be given "fullness in Christ?" What is God talking about here for you and me? If we live and minister in His fullness, what would that look like for us daily?

For the apostle Paul, that surely meant a fullness of adequacy. Jesus was his resource for ministry. It meant also a fullness of confidence for a man who often struggled with weakness and fear. The fullness of Christ meant power and strength for Paul as he faced demands that far exceeded his own abilities, and it brought comfort in the midst of pain and affliction. It surely meant a fullness of righteousness before a holy God, and the fullness of God's glorious presence surrounding him, even as we saw with the prophets. Jesus' fullness provided wisdom for Paul when he was confused and when he had difficulty figuring out what God was doing or why things were happening as they were. The fullness of Christ was all of Paul's hope in ministry.

I think there was another aspect of the "fullness of Christ" that kept Paul's heart and enabled him to keep going in the kind of ministry described here. I believe there was a sufficiency in Jesus that filled Paul's heart to overflowing. A sufficiency of joy, a fullness of satisfaction, a measure of wholeness was given to Paul in Christ that left no sense of emptiness in any way or on any level. I think Jesus Himself was enough for him.

Therefore, the great apostle Paul, the very one who said "Follow my example, as I follow the example of Christ" (1 Cor. 11:1), did not need success in ministry to be fulfilled. He did not depend on the responses of people or the affirmation of his peers. He did not need money; he did not need numbers of any kind; he did not need political power; there was nothing he had to win. He did not need physical comfort or sexual fulfillment out of God's will. Paul did not need to build a kingdom in his name because Jesus was sufficient to fill him up.

## CHRIST'S FULLNESS IN ME

Do we really believe this great truth of the Scriptures? Do we actually live with a sense of Christ's fullness from day to day? What about your own heart? Is Jesus truly enough to fill you up in every way? Let me share what the fullness of Christ has meant to me.

My father introduced me to pornography when I was fourteen years old. He modeled before me a lifestyle of unfaithfulness in his marriage to my mother and encouraged me to follow him as one whose sexual desires were out of control. I became a Christian three years later, but for several years I struggled with pornography and the paralyzing guilt and shame that accompany that devastating fruit of this dark world.

God has healed my heart in His redemption through Christ, and His redemption has overflowed into every area of my life. Let me share with you something of God's healing process in which He set me free to be His servant.

- God opened my understanding to the "united with Christ" experience that Paul describes in Romans 6:1-11, one in which I shared in His death and resurrection and am now dead to sin and alive to God.
- The power which flows from Christ living within me has enabled me to live a life pleasing to the Lord.
- God's holiness was the vision that called me onward and caused me to hunger for holiness in my own life.
- The love of Christ compelled me to obedience. Rather than the manipulation of guilt and fear, God wooed me to freedom and intimacy with Him through His wonderful giving, forgiving, accepting love.
- God gave me a beautiful wife. Karen's love for me leaves no desires unfulfilled.
- I found that Jesus was sufficient to fill every longing of my heart and every empty place in my life. It was the fullness of Christ, His love, His joy and His satisfaction of every spiritual and sensory need in my entire being that gave me a measure of wholeness which enabled me to function as a full person and as a full minister of God's grace.

## THE MARKS OF FINISHING WELL

We are living in a day when many men and women are "beginning well" in the ministry but not many are "finishing well." So many of our brothers and our sisters began their work with a genuine call from God and a deep commitment to serve Him. Their faith was sincere and their love for God was sacrificial. Their highest desire was to give themselves for Christ and His kingdom, but along the way, the pressures, the pain, the disappointments and the failures of life, many of which we have discussed in this book, have caused them to burn out, to lose heart and to give up.

It was the fullness of Christ that enabled Paul to finish well. At the end of his third missionary journey, as he was on his way to Jerusalem, he stopped at Miletus and called for the elders at Ephesus to meet him there. He had ministered at Ephesus for three years, and this church was very dear to his heart. In his closing exhortation to the elders at Ephesus, we see the characteristics that enabled him to walk in the works that God had ordained for him from the foundation of the world and to fulfill the ministry that God had entrusted to him. It is these same character qualities, flowing out of the fullness of Christ, which will also enable you and me to "finish well" and to walk gloriously in the works that our Father has planned for us.

## Integrity and Character

> From Miletus, Paul sent to Ephesus for the elders of the church. When they arrived, he said to them: "You know how I lived the whole time I was with you, from the first day I came into the province of Asia. I served the Lord with great humility and with tears, although I was severely tested by the plots of the Jews." (Acts 20:17-19)

Paul's integrity and character were well known within the church at Ephesus. He said, "You know how I lived the whole time I was with you." This confidence was the foundation for the message he now brought to the elders. The character and integrity which flows from us as godly men and women will be the foundation for our ministries as well. Are these qualities the first that we seek for those who would serve in God's Church today? It seems that we often seek and even train first for proficiency of skills in preaching, leading or technology and then we hope that the integrity is there as well. For Paul, and for those who seek God's glory in His Church, it is of first importance.

## Humility

Paul walked humbly before the Lord and before His people. Like John the Baptist, Paul had the grace to see himself through the eyes of God. John knew who he was and he knew who he wasn't. John knew he was not the Christ, but he was the one sent to be a witness to the Light. True humility is not seeing ourselves for less than what we are; rather, it is a confident affirmation of who God has made us to be in Christ and the ministry He has set before us. We get into trouble when we see ourselves out of proportion—as more than who God says we are or as less than He sees us to be.

## Intimate Relationships

*You know that I have not hesitated to preach anything that would be helpful to you but have taught you publicly and from house to house. (Acts 20:20)*

Paul shared intimate relationships with his people. Earlier he said that he served with tears. Here he described the way he taught them publicly and from house to house. He was with the people and his heart went out to them and was open to them as well. Paul was knowable, touchable, available, and able to be moved deeply by their needs and their cries.

## Message of Repentance and Faith

*I have declared to both Jews and Greeks that they must turn to God in repentance and have faith in our Lord Jesus. (Acts 20:21)*

Paul's message was repentance and faith. He called all hearers to turn from their sins and from any hope other than God's work through His Son at Calvary and to turn to Christ in faith, placing all of their hopes in His blood shed on the cross.

## Obedient to Death

*And now, compelled by the Spirit, I am going to Jerusalem, not knowing what will happen to me there. I only know that in every city the Holy Spirit warns me that prison and hardships are facing me. (Acts 20:22,23)*

Paul was obedient to the point of death. He continued to follow the leading of God's Spirit, knowing that afflictions, pain, persecu-tions, prison and even death were before him.

## Endurance to the End

*However, I consider my life worth nothing to me, if only I may finish the race and complete the task the Lord Jesus has given me—the task of testifying to the gospel of God's grace. Now I know that none of you among whom I have gone about preaching the kingdom will ever see me again. (Acts 20:24,25)*

Paul endured to the end. Endurance may well be the most important character quality in ministry. Paul was committed to finishing his race whatever the cost. He did not bail out in the face of overwhelming obstacles because he knew God was there and was able to keep his heart.

## Proclamation of God's Whole Counsel

*Therefore, I declare to you today that I am innocent of the blood of all men. For I have not hesitated to proclaim to you the whole will of God. (Acts 20:26,27)*

Paul proclaimed the whole counsel of God. The basis of his innocence before the Lord was his faithfulness to the entire message God had entrusted to him. He did not preach pet themes or speak on interesting topics that he thought might draw an audience, or pull out a verse here or there that might serve as a reinforcement for an idea that gripped his fancy. He taught all of the Scriptures as a framework for the Holy Spirit's ministry to the people of God.

## A Watchman over His Heart

> *Keep watch over yourselves and all the flock of which the Holy Spirit has made you overseers. Be shepherds of the church of God, which he bought with his own blood. (Acts 20:28)*

Paul kept watch over his own heart. He guarded his attitudes, affections, motives and desires. Paul was not deceived by the enemy into thinking that he was above the things that caused others to fall. Many pastors and missionaries get into trouble when they start believing the good things that their people say about them. After months, or even years, of hearing, "You are so wonderful, so spiritual, so sensitive or so 'whatever,' " we often begin to believe that foolishness. We love living on that pedestal, and soon we think we really are different than others and not vulnerable to falling into sexual or financial sin, or other things that would bring disgrace on the name of our Lord.

There is another side to this battle as well. Other pastors and leaders get into trouble when their people do not give them the respect that they deserve or do not affirm them or care for them financially. Perhaps we are compared to the great television or radio preachers, as we discussed earlier, and are found wanting in the eyes of our people. We need to guard our hearts from anger, jealousy and bitterness in these times.

## A Watchman over God's Flock

> *I know that after I leave, savage wolves will come in among you and will not spare the flock. Even from your own number men*

*will arise and distort the truth in order to draw away disciples after them. So be on your guard! Remember that for three years I never stopped warning each of you night and day with tears. (Acts 20:29-31)*

Paul kept watch over the flock of God. We have been made overseers of God's Church, His people purchased with His own blood. Savage wolves will come, even from within. There are those who distort the truth about God's Word and even the truth about us and our ministries. Others try to draw followers to themselves. Paul urged the church at Ephesus to "make every effort to keep the unity of the spirit through the bond of peace" (Eph. 4:3). Divisions in the Church are rampant today and a powerful tool of the enemy. Satan's deceptions are incredibly powerful. More churches are split on the basis of "rightness" than on any other issue. Satan does not care who is right. He loves "rightness!" The Pharisees were the most "right" people in the world, but their hearts were far from God. We quickly forget that it is our love for one another which reveals that we have come from Jesus (John 13:34,35), and it is our unity which reveals that Jesus has been sent by the Father (John 17:23). We are called to guard the flock of God from the destroyers and the dividers.

## Message—God's Grace

*Now I commit you to God and to the word of his grace, which can build you up and give you an inheritance among all those who are sanctified. (Acts 20:32)*

Paul's message was the grace of God. Again, the ministry of God's Word was preeminent in Paul's heart, and these Scriptures bring us to an understanding of His grace. It is our Father's loving, merciful, gracious giving which sets us free to walk in holiness. There is no religious structure or legalistic system that can bring the people of God to loving obedience. Only the freedom of His grace moves us to the service He desires.

## A Servant's Heart

*I have not coveted anyone's silver or gold or clothing. You yourselves know that these hands of mine have supplied my own needs and the needs of my companions. In everything I did, I showed you that by this kind of hard work we must help the weak, remembering the words the Lord Jesus himself said: "It is more blessed to give than to receive." (Acts 20:33-35)*

Paul modeled the heart of a servant. We are greatly in need of men and women whose ministries are filled with character and integrity. These are attitudes of the heart and are expressed in serving. These qualities are seen most vividly in our attitudes concerning finances. God has not called us to build our lives at the expense of the sheep, but to build up His sheep even at the cost of our very lives. In a world of users, takers and consumers, God has raised us up to be givers, as we follow not only Jesus' words but also His own example .

*For even the Son of Man did not come to be served, but to serve, and to give his life as a ransom for many. (Mark 10:45)*

May God give us the grace to "finish well," to persevere even to the end for the sake of His name and the building of His Church. Above all, may we hunger to hear those words, "Well done, good and faithful servant," as we stand before His throne. May His glorious presence that kept us from day to day be our joy and delight for all eternity!

## REFLECTIONS, COMMITMENTS AND PRAYER

*Lord, I know that only You will be able to keep me to the end and enable me to finish well in the work You have committed to me. Would You teach me again and again to rely on the resources of Christ who lives within me and to put no confidence in my own abilities? May the fullness of Christ satisfy my every longing and set me free to be Your servant alone. By Your grace, may I stand before Your glorious throne at the end of my race and hear those words, "Well done."*

# Scripture Index

# Our Goal

We believe that God's people hunger to experience Him in a way that is genuine, life transforming, and ever-deepening. This hunger is not satisfied with a "how to", formulistic approach to life. It is not satisfied with a theology which remains detached from life. Nor is it satisfied with experiences which have no grounding in the Scriptures.

Rather, we believe that God satisfied our deepest longings through a set of intimate relationships: with Himself, with His Word, and His people.

Leadership Resources desires to bring God's people into an encounter with God exalted in His holiness, sovereignty, glory and grace, through an in-depth exposure to His life-giving Word which will encourage, cleanse, and transform God's people. We seek to deepen commitments within a local body of believers and to encourage restoration of damaged relationships. We seek to instill a renewed passion for God's eternal purposes, so that all the earth might be filled with His glory.

# Leadership Resources International

Leadership Resources is a ministry of discipleship for churches and church leaders. We provide conferences, leadership training and materials designed to assist churches in the work of equipping their people for ministry. Our conferences in the area of discipleship, ministry, family, relationships and Inductive Bible Study are available to churches and mission organizations throughout the world.

The materials we produce are designed for personal use, one–to–one discipleship, Sunday School classes, home Bible studies and family ministries. Some of our studies are also published in Spanish.

For more information about our conferences or materials, contact:

Leadership Resources
12575 South Ridgeland Avenue
Palos Heights, IL 60463
(800) 980–2226

LRI@Leadershipresources.org